D1084692

Illustrated with drawings by the author

E. P. DUTTON, INC. | NEW YORK

Published in the United States by
E. P. Dutton, Inc. 2 Park Avenue, New York, N.Y. 10016

Library of Congress Cataloging in Publication Data

Lee, Laurel.
Mourning into dancing.
1. Lee, Laurel. 2. Divorced mothers—United States—Biography.
3. Remarriage—United States. I. Title.
HQ759.L43 1984 306.8'9'0924 83-25384

ISBN: 0-525-24250-3

Published simultaneously in Canada
by Fitzhenry & Whiteside Limited, Toronto

Designed by Mark O'Connor

10 9 8 7 6 5 4 3 2 1

First Edition

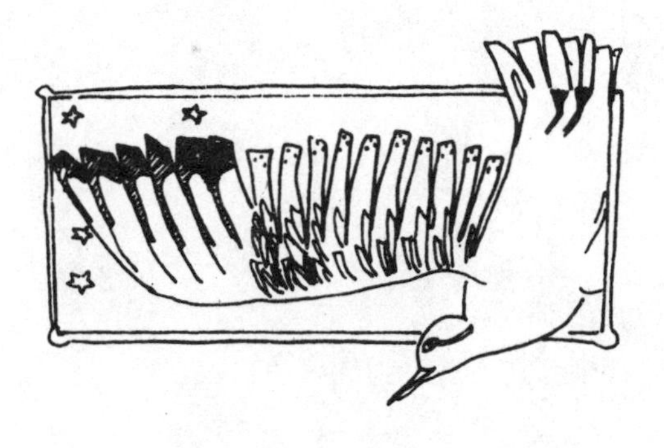

It's about time that Mary Lou Kelly and Dee Dee Smith rode together on the dedication horse. Thank you Sherri Crumpler, the Schleighs, Pat, Bob, Judy, Sally R., Lorraine Sughrue. Saluting Barbara who typed and Rodney who saved for us the expired code date cheese.

There's a thousand hands I know that deserve a dedication page ring publicly slipped upon your finger. But what is this spot of mist compared to the mounted and cut jewel in the sky?

Portland, Oregon May 1980

Standing in the hall, I had finished turning off all but the bathroom light. The end of its glow reached back to the three children's bedrooms. While I was just looking in at them, the youngest turned in her sleep. My perception was of them lying in their beds growing. Cells were doubling, legs lengthening, bangs reaching over eyebrows for a lash. I wondered if the lighted fluorescent panel wasn't one of my substitutes for safety that a father's presence can lend to a house at night. One thought, built in a sigh, seemed almost audible; it will soon be five years that they have lived with one adult.

Crossing the pine wood floor, I entered the smallest and darkest of the four bedrooms. It was originally designed to be nothing more than an enclosed porch, a place for houseplants. Because of the number of small paned windows, the sound of the rain seemed louder, as if a fleck of metal had suddenly become encased in every drop.

I thought of how quickly the time had passed since my husband first deserted us. "Before the Divorce" and "After the Divorce" had become my personal markers of time. It was shortly after the birth of Mary Elisabeth. The pregnancy had been complicated by the discovery that I had a lymphatic cancer. I remembered the shock of seeing the visible proof in a routine chest X ray. To my untrained eye, the tumor had looked like a white deflated balloon hanging next to my lung. Refusing the professional recommendation of an abortion, I had carried the child through upper-mantle radiation therapy.

I could still visualize the page from my medical chart. The doctor had written, "We don't have much time left with this patient." There had been three preschoolers then, and my husband Richard had staggered under the potential load of raising them himself. He had already remarried by the time I came home in remission.

I longed to dissolve the memories into sleep, but my thoughts seemed to be increasing in volume instead of fading into mists. This reciting of history has its own momentum, I mused.

The period of health had lasted a brief eighteen months before a new tumor was discovered in my spine. Chemotherapy effected a second remission, but there was still one doctor's ringing warning of relapse: "Laurel, you only have a twenty percent chance of a five-year survival rate."

I tossed in my bed looking for a new crevice in my pillow, while my displaced feet absorbed the cold between the sheets.

"I've now known eleven months of health!"

Like a familiar roll call, I began to enumerate the symptoms:

"Any night sweats?"

"No."

"Any swollen lymph nodes?"

"No."

"What about back pains?"

"Sometimes."

I had caught up to the present, but my mind still wouldn't rest. It wanted the future too. I remembered my son Matthew's question:

"If you die, what will happen to me and the girls?" I could feel a band of tension cross my chest. There is no thought without a corresponding feeling. Every serious meditation seemed to begin and end with a cry for their welfare.

Raising up for a minute on my elbow, I looked outside. The wind sounded as if it had been caught in the pine tree. There was nothing but darkness. No streetlamp reached back to the yard, nor was a neighbor using any visible electricity. I shut my eyes, wanting to cry.

Prayer seemed to be my only flagpole. With haste I fastened to it every petition, including my cry for a husband. The request seemed frayed by the years of me mounting it with every other colored need and watching it rise out of sight.

In the early morning, I turned over the fragments of last night's dreams. Only small parts remained, like prehistoric art that has almost faded into the cave's wall. A pressure on my shoulder made me open my eyes. It was Mary Elisabeth, who comes to my bed as her first station upon rising. Being too young for school, she consistently refuses her privilege to sleep in order to visit me. The label on her nightgown is a white tab standing up at her neck. Frequent launderings have faded its statement of fabric content and care. The only words that remain are its foreign origin of Taiwan.

"I want to eat!"

My daughter had hunger to think about. She has decisions to make on her choice of cereal boxes. She has consumer issues to debate on the necessity of white sugar for her breakfast seasoning.

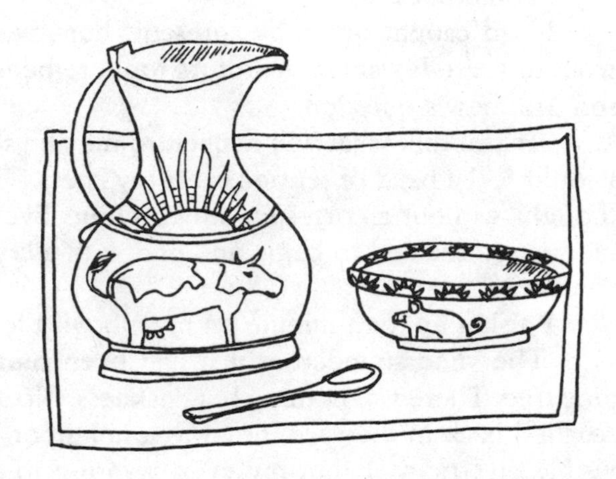

"Mother!"

Raising my knees under my blanket puts a mountain range across my quilt. I think the word "No" must be a one-syllable sound in most languages. It requires frequent use.

A quick glance at my watch makes me jump up. Her older brother and sister, obliged to rise for school, still lie locked in their blankets. While pushing open the children's doors, I wondered if I still defined the routines of motherhood as the bones that gave my life its shape.

"Wake up, Anna."

She says "No," and does it.

"Matthew, get up now!"

He says he will and goes back to sleep. His bed is a magnet and his pajamas have turned to steel.

Even after their last grooming and departure, I stood on the front porch not caring if a barefoot woman in an oversize flannel nightgown was appropriate for neighborhood viewing. The morning was bright, rare weather after the rainstorms of spring. Portland, Oregon, should be the headquarters for manufacturing the umbrellas of the world.

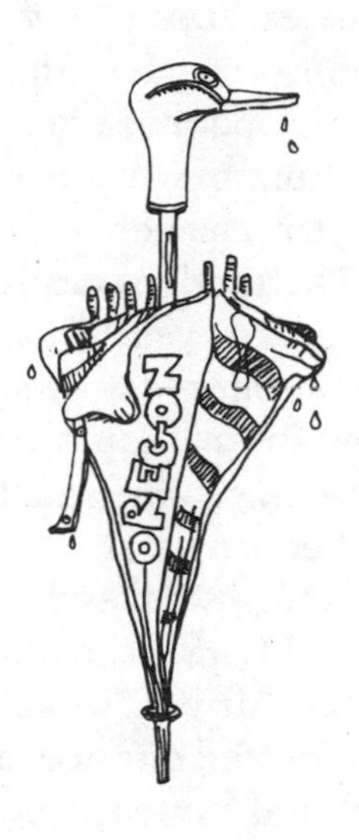

While staring into the neighbor's bed of daffodils I began to feel like a shepherdess held in place by a flock of emotions. I recognized that loneliness brushed the closest to my legs. Not wanting to hear any plaintive bleats from melancholy, my eye pulled up to scan the row of well-kept lawns on Couch Street before going inside. The houses, built at the turn of the century, had second stories and front porches. Most of the residents were retired, and our purchase was the beginning of children coming back into the neighborhood. I felt we were violating them with our rollerskates and voices that required exclamation points as punctuation.

I didn't pause at the kitchen sink, or by the stairwell that led to every unmade bed, but went right to my desk. It was littered with envelopes. Most were from cancer patients, while a very few were invitations to speak at women's groups, or various civic organizations.

Publishing my two diaries had allowed me to visit some of the galaxies beyond my home planet of thrift stores and canning jars. For the random occasion of speaking into a microphone, I had purchased a dress suit uniform. I could number my trips by counting the receipts from the dry cleaners who purged my skirt of luncheon spots. The random airplane tickets fulfilled my secret love of a trip. For years I had entered every supermarket contest that offered a destination as its prize.

Putting a pen in my mouth, I quickly removed it as soon as my tongue traced the small indentation of an old toothmark. I looked down at my appointment calendar, opened to the coming weekend.

"Dear Ladies," I practiced out loud. "I was once the wife of a school bus driver. I had fifteen dollars a week for groceries. We heated our house with wood. I had two small children, found myself pregnant with a third and could never stop coughing. . . ."

After suggesting dinner in a neighborhood café, the children jostled each other down the steps to our station wagon. They always approach the car loudly contesting for the front seat. I've instituted a rule of taking turns for the coveted spot, so their arguments are modified from "I want it," to "It's my turn!" I won little peace with my law. Anna gets it. Next to me, my daughter appears carved from a bar of Ivory soap. She is eight years old, small and white.

Mary Elisabeth crawls in the back with her doll. All possible attentions for wardrobe and hairstyling are lavished on her eight-inch polyurethane baby. She asks me if she can marry her playmate on the block when she grows up. Anna snickers, and Matthew calls her "dumb." Before he finishes pronouncing the judgment, Mary Elisabeth is protesting.

I use my automatic words for requesting quiet, while thinking that I didn't know I had nerves until I had children.

"No one speak for three blocks!"

At the restaurant table, Anna outlines a whole new line of popsicles for public consumption. A school project on nutrition has inspired her vision of vegetable pops.

"Each one could have a french fry, carrot stick, or celery slice frozen down the middle."

Matthew's idea of merchandising doesn't go beyond the needs of a family. He requests cereal popsicles—milk and Cheerios quintessentially frozen in the ice cube tray for tomorrow's breakfast.

I noticed Matthew's conversations were becoming less concerned with wanting a father. Our one-parent family was becoming a fact, not a complaint. Of the children he had mourned our loss the most. We had buried certain hopes, but never "Hope" itself.

After passing the catsup and blotting another spilled drink with wads of napkins, I reminded them again that tomorrow I was going to Southern California to be a speaker at a women's retreat. The girls groaned with a sound identical to their morning cry when I approach with the hairbrush.

"I'll only be gone a couple of days. You'll each be going to your other house."

Each child had their own family where they could stay during any of my overnight absences. They were all homes with a father. Glad for support, I thought of it as part of their education, like music and swimming lessons, to be exposed to daily living in a house with a man.

Matthew demanded to know everything I was going to do in Los Angeles. I suspected he wanted to be assured that I wouldn't be visiting Disneyland without them.

"The only extra thing I will be doing is having dinner with a man who makes films."

Their responding exclamation emphasized "Movies!" not the fact that I was having a very rare date.

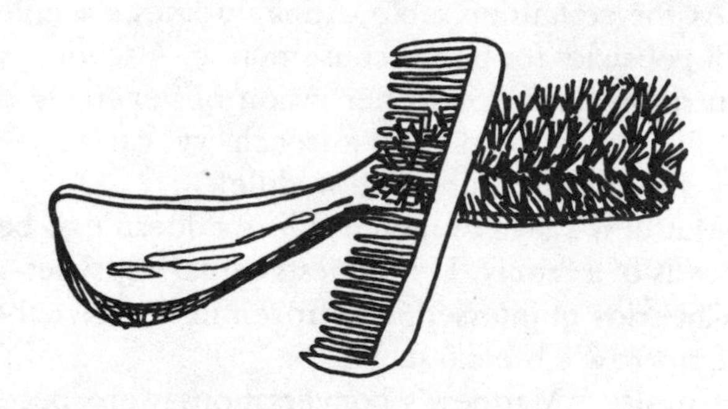

Los Angeles, May 10

In countless mirrors of public bathrooms, I have been amused at the reflection of women who fought with a single hair as if the outcome of their beauty depended on their comb's victory. Whatever judgment I gave those faces, it returned to me in the women's room of the Hilton Hotel. Thinking, "Only death will unlock this sidecar of vanity," I went back to the lobby to wait for the arrival of my dinner date.

I could have written my three encounters with Jeremy Foster on a fingernail, as they were small and concise. I met him the first time three years ago. He was one of a million hands I felt I had shaken in all the introductions at a national booksellers' convention. The following year we nodded across the room to each other during a convention banquet. Last summer we were seated side by side at a publishers' business dinner. Through those years I had heard others speak with the greatest respect of his work in distributing feature films that had a religious content.

My stored impressions could hardly recall any of our dialogue, or his visible features, except he had a mustache. It's what I couldn't see that I remembered. I had thought of him as a well that gave us clear water from some depth.

I waited for Jeremy Foster at a book rack by the hotel sundry shop. I was looking at the number of gothic novels whose covers showed women running in billowing capes from darkened cliffside castles.

Somehow, I knew exactly when Jeremy approached me. I don't know if I detected his presence in an outer field of my peripheral vision, or from a vibration on the carpet that only a foot with a thin leather sole could sense. Yet I pivoted, fully expecting him.

He stood a few feet from me with a most amiable expression of greeting.

Walking toward him I felt a warmth best expressed in a quick hug.

"You've cut your hair," he said.

I knew if we had only shaken hands, he wouldn't have uttered his observation.

"I decided I was getting too old at thirty-four to hold it back with barrettes."

As we walked outside to his car, I measured Jeremy's stature by judging the total number of inches that he towered over my head. He was tall and broad, as if it took twice the clay to form him.

He had parked on the circular driveway by the front entrance. Taking a ring of keys from his jacket pocket, he fitted it to the lock of a large red Mercedes-Benz. All of the door buttons rose simultaneously with the precision of a German equation. Instinctively, I knew no small children had ever written letter "O's" on his back window with fingers wet with french fries. I've always felt a certain sympathy for those who are fated to own expensive configurations for transportation. It's the extra burden of protecting chrome and shine from inevitable damages. A car that is seasoned by injuries has a certain freedom from automotive cares.

I uttered, "It resembles a tomato soup can," out of sympathy for the burden of its maintenance.

His quick smile seemed to have a question mark set into his cheek: "What does that mean?"

There was something about him that wanted me to form explanations using the essences of things. I remained silent in respect to the fact we had only been together for seven minutes.

But yet, I thought how each human being could be compared to a lake with private shallows and depths. It's up on the shoreline that everything visible is cast: Mercedes car grilles and business cards.

The restaurant was designed by someone born in Los Angeles. The management's concept of formal dress was clean sport clothes. All the busboys wore shorts.

Jeremy asked my menu preference and gave it himself to the waiter. He was of that old order that helped women with doors and coat sleeves. Unlike me, he showed no disdain for the bread, but rather a marked enthusiasm for its ample serving and the linen wrap that kept it warm. I suspended my spearing of a cherry tomato to watch him. Jeremy was lavish with the butter, much like a modern painter covering a canvas with thick spots of yellow oil.

Seated at tables around us were girls packaged in long dresses with knots of flowers at their waist or throat. It was the season's fresh beauties crossing into the world through the tape of the senior prom.

I asked Jeremy what new movie he was working on.

"There are several, but that is the language of Los Angeles," he answered.

I mentioned a dialect of Portland.

"It's vegetable gardens and what seed to plant after all danger of frost has passed." Jeremy laughed while adding: "In Minnesota, where I was raised, it's sport tags and the animal whose life is in jeopardy during hunting season."

I went back to a new version of my first query.

"Why do you make movies?"

I was aware that, unwillingly, a kind of radar screen had automatically gone into operation. It is a faculty of all single women. I thought of questions that would delve into Jeremy's motives, which are a more accurate measure of a man than what he owns.

Jeremy was quiet for a long time. I could feel him sorting phrases.

"I couldn't imagine doing anything else. It's the potential of the medium that I love."

His voice seemed to turn inward, and neither did he look at me. It made me imagine words built with clouds.

"It's the beauty of being able to communicate wholesome values, Laurel."

"You are a lonely manufacturer," I replied, while thinking of all the ads on the entertainment page.

Jeremy rubbed his forehead above his eyebrow.

"It's true," he answered.

"When I look at most scripts, there seem to be more possibilities for cinema in taping household appliances, toasting bread or cleaning rugs."

"Why do you publish books, Laurel?"

Unlike him, I answered quickly without measuring my reply:

"Because it's a developed form of putting a message in a bottle, and casting it to sea."

As dinner arrived, Jeremy went on to describe the stories that his company was planning for films. They were all movies for families. I sat respecting him for not reading to me from his own back chapters. I knew he was divorced. It's many an escort at dinner who wants to read his old dialogues of a marriage dissolution. Such men conclude their paragraph with the expectation of winning another critic of their ex-spouse. I found Jeremy to be more noble than that. He was animated with ideas.

"Bluntly speaking, Laurel, if I don't use films to bellow truth I feel I'm another accomplice to liars and forgers."

He paused only to give his steak consideration. He invited me to perceive his plate as an extension of my own and began to separate a portion for me to taste.

It was at that moment Jeremy asked me about my health.

"You've had Hodgkin's disease?"

He didn't provide a pause for any nod from me.

"How long have you been in remission?"

"Eleven months."

Jeremy lifted his eyes and momentarily locked them with mine. I thought of how the phrase "almost a year" rhymed with "so near, some fear, my dear."

"You're finished with it," he said with a tone of authority.

"It's not always that simple," I answered. My words were gray compared to his black-and-white declarative. My response contained the minute single cell that could divide into a disagreement.

Jeremy asked for dessert menus, changing the subject.

"We'll have to arrange more dinners together, Laurel."

My reply had more under the surface than on top.

"It's not often I meet someone who I can really talk to."

My casual tone helped conceal the fact that there were no men in my life with whom I shared any conversational depths.

In the drive back to my accommodations, we opened our appointment calendars. Jeremy had a leather-bound book with the year written in gold script. My calendar, the size of a checkbook, was a free gift to anyone who walked into the neighborhood bank during December. The next week in the life of Jeremy Foster included appointments in New York, Washington, D.C., Virginia, and Toronto. In thirteen days I was flying to London with Matthew for a book promotion. The fact was engraved in our own writing: We didn't have time on our side.

For me, our conversation didn't seem to end. Portions of phrases kept reappearing for a mental replay long after we had separated. Finally, I decided to reprimand my thoughts with discipline. I shouted through the walls of my mind.

"Quiet!"

"Take your seat, Affection, for you are out of place!"

With the tone of a teacher turning to the blackboard, I lectured:

"Let us remember what it is like to be deserted. The

fact is, you've had cancer twice. And that, coupled with the care of young children, makes any relationship beyond friends impossible."

As a chalk stick would print in capitals, I stated:

"YOU ARE UNDESIRABLE!"

Then imagination sketched my self-image to weigh 300 pounds, with loose teeth and mysteriously missing eyebrows.

Portland, May 14

My robot body knew its track of chores through the house and neighborhood. My laundry basket continued in its own magic of never being able to be emptied. My toothbrush lecture still had to be delivered at night.

After my evening with Jeremy, I thought of the men in my life. Most of them I had met at my local church, with first names exchanged in the perimeter of a congregational pew. Some had a need to continually define the relationship, providing for themselves a measure of safety. Those ended or began sentences naming me "Sister." It gave our family a lot of brothers, and I didn't press beyond it.

I had a drawer full of letters from men, too. A certain sample sent me their picture with a prominent return address. Some had more to offer in common compatibility than our mutual singleness: they had cancer.

I thought of Ellis Johnson who always sits in the front row on Sunday morning. Once he confided he kept a box filled with recipes that he clipped from the newspaper for the woman who would become his wife. He was in love with a girl in the choir who had asked her parents for canning jars for her birthday. There's a principle for marriage in the partners being evenly yoked.

I knew I needed another woman's opinion on life and love. After dialing Arlene, I balanced the receiver between my shoulder and ear. My kitchen sink has the added perspective of a window, and a phone with a maximum extension cord. At my ring, my friend had already completed her breakfast plates, but allocated her phone time to sponging off the exterior of her appliances.

"I met someone special," I said.

Once spoken, it seemed to be a sentence hung with all manner of hopes and fears.

I could tell that Arlene had put down her cleaning rag. Her voice lost its waver of kitchen action.

She interrupted my narrative in the middle of a sentence.

"Stop defining his soul to me. I want some external details. What's his age?"

"I think Jeremy is about thirteen years older."

"Does he have children?"

"Yes, but I don't know their ages, or how many."

My friend was taking a single syllable and humming it in between my answers. They felt like punctuations of doubt.

"Arlene, someday I would like to know the experience of a committed marriage relationship, even against the odds of illness and children. I know there are a lot of men in my own congregation who would make a solid husband. But I've always hesitated to encourage any relationship there because I know their expectations for a wife could have narrow perimeters. They wouldn't want a partner who would like the freedom to collect elastic bands from used airport destination cards.

"Jeremy is the first man I've met who shares with me all the same ethics of faith, yet is active with a global vision in making Christian films."

"Just how important is his 'professionalism' to you, Laurel?"

My immediate silence confessed to vanity. There was such a contrast between Jeremy and my husband, who had once supported us by hanging soap samples from the knobs of Portland's front doors.

"No," I could finally answer truthfully. "It is his qualities of character that draw me."

"Well, I hope he likes you with an enthusiasm equal to your own. I just want you to be careful, Laurel."

I thanked her, hung up, and stared at the pattern of a quilt in a prepasted scrubbable vinyl wall covering.

I knew Arlene could trace my history. We had met at college seventeen years ago. Her ear, alone, had heard details that had been hidden from others. It was to her I confided that my ex-husband had been ordered by the court to pay $150 a month for child support. She had sent by gallons of milk when he never gave us anything, and I was unable to consider employment because of the daily radiation treatments. The money I had borrowed from my parents was only enough to finance a one-room apartment.

I remembered the anguish. There was a night after the children fell asleep that I had called their father to ask when he was going to send us a check. My issue was loaves of bread. He replied that there would never be a check and threatened to fight for legal custody of the children if I went to any authority for my rights.

He said, "You are a fourth-stage cancer patient, and in a law court they would be awarded to me. In the last nine months, you've had seven hospitalizations. . . ."

I hung up the phone trembling. The baby's crib was in the closet and she had turned in her bed while I was talking. I looked up at Matthew asleep on the closet shelf, proud that his bed resembled a train berth. Anna had filled my side of the mattress with her stuffed animals. Her dark hair was drifting across her cheek. Fighting the terror of what to do, I piled the toys on the floor and climbed between the covers.

I knew that I would never do anything that could risk my losing the children.

In some state, neither in the folds of sleep nor awake, I tossed all night full of images of trying to find my way. Running down narrow streets I didn't know, caught in a

woods without a destination, the pictures inverted and changed. At dawn I sat up, wishing the sky had a door that I could just walk through and rest.

Still asleep, Anna had turned toward me. The pillow had extended from her head to the upper portion of her chest. I remembered whispering out loud in such a low voice that it was barely audible, "I will not destroy myself with bitterness."

It was Arlene who said, "You'll have to get welfare temporarily."

Then, she reminded me that there is beauty for ashes, and mourning can be turned into dancing.

May 15

Once last Autumn I found a brick chimney in the basement. Its function was to act as an exhaust pipe for the central oil furnace. Its path to the roof was behind the kitchen wall that was used as a backdrop for my refrigerator.

The chimney seemed imprisoned behind lath and plaster. I wanted to release the craggy red bricks for public view. I pulled the icebox out to the back porch with the help of some brothers. Borrowing a crowbar, I was a controlled vandal beating through the wall studs and filler. When the remodeling was finished, the refrigerator was never returned from its relocation out the back door.

I was outside on my knees wiping out the two bottom bins when the telephone rang. I resented it interrupting my study on the effects of aging on forgotten, single vegetables. Old lettuce leaves meld into the porcelain, while geriatric carrots display enormous pliability. The quality of the phone's intermittent rings ranged from the first sound that seemed polite, to a demand to be answered. Some of the chill in the icebox duplicated its frost in my "Hello."

It was Jeremy. He was dialing from one of the lobbies of the world. He asked if I had tasted the bratwurst sausages in the pedestrian corridors at O'Hare Airport. He was building sentences that reminded me of small even numbers. He asked about the weather. The dialogues like multifigured equations are conversations composed of invisible substances, the gusts of philosophy that blow all life.

Our exchange ran its course down to the small pat sentences of severing. In a lower-pitched voice, as an amended postscript, Jeremy asked if it would be acceptable with me for him to route himself through Portland to Los Angeles.

"Will you book a suitable hotel for me for the weekend?"

"I will," was my tiny reply.

Back staring at the racks of my refrigerator, my emotions were at a continental divide. Besides the anticipation of a visit with him, one set of feelings flowed into the sea of not wanting him to come at all. I feared jeopardizing a new friendship. Controlled dinners at some distance seemed much safer in contrast to our own nightly round of spilled milk.

A tapping on the sidewalk interrupted my meditation. Melanie Parker came to the back door with her youngest daughter in tow. The child's hair was gathered for the day on top of her head by a rubber band, looking like a small palm tree riding over her forehead.

I put on a kettle and got down my tin of Leningrad black tea. While sucking the steam from the mugs, waiting to take sips, I asked Melanie how she was doing.

Like me, she was a single mother who had her two older children in the same school mine attended. There was almost a club of us at church, a group within a group.

We overlapped each other's Saturday evenings, and shared an occasional holiday.

"I've met someone," I said, "and just now he called to say he is coming to visit us in Portland."

My tone emphasized the words *"just now."*

After one audible sigh, Melanie asked for some honey. Filling the spoon with the caramel-colored crystals she lowered them just below the surface and watched them dissolve. Her plaid flannel shirt had smudges of dried paint on the sleeve.

She supported her children by doing exterior house painting. Her specialty was Victorian properties with any lace woodwork trimmed in a contrasting color. It was only on Sunday that her clothes were free from spots of enamel.

"I just can't imagine myself complicating my life further by deciding to like someone."

Putting down my own cup I looked at Melanie, marveling at her detachment. To most, matrimony was a silvery cage on the landscape. It seemed that many who were in it wished to be out, while those who were single spent much time finding their right entrance.

Melanie continued: "Well, the fact he's coming to visit certainly indicates interest. Because of the children, all of our situations are complex, but yours is more so."

If words could take hues, Melanie's implications seemed to project the yellow-colored caution of traffic signals.

"It's true, Melanie, that any man that would consider marrying me has the risk that he could someday be a single father to my children. What's good about that is it creates an ultimate character test for any suitor."

Melanie started laughing, then quoted Proverbs:

Many a man claims to have unfailing love, but a faithful man who can find?

At dinner, I made it into a story for the children. I waited until all of their ice cream that exceeded appetite had long melted into sticky pools.

"There was once a gypsy girl," I said.

Only Anna focused on me. The other two were busy creating sun rays by drawing their spoons out from the remains of their dessert.

"She met the headmaster of another wagon train at a fire some distance from her camp. He played a violin, and his music was the first she had heard that she felt she could dance to. . . ."

"Next time, buy chocolate sauce," interrupted Mary Elisabeth. After voicing her request she put the handle of her spoon in her mouth and plucked the other end like a primitive musical instrument.

Silenced, I began to gather the dishes. It was my action equivalent to lowering the American flag at day's end. As the rectangle of stripes is folded over onto the stars, I placed the three plates on top of the fourth which wobbled with crushed chicken bones.

Later, I couldn't sleep. There seemed to be scented air coming through the open window. The breeze penetrated more than my senses, finding passage to an inner restlessness. I went out to the backyard and stood between the two large pine trees at the back fence. Enough light was cast from a neighbor's porch that it illuminated Matthew's rusting yellow dump truck parked on a swell of roots. My arms began to swing in wide strokes, resembling a conductor powerless to keep them still before the orchestra. I leaped from one foot to another, gaining momentum. Spinning on my toes, I unclipped my single barrette, so my hair could duplicate all motion at my shoulders. Only when there was a need for deep breaths did I rest.

Father of all gypsies,
From the ends of the earth
Cry I, unto You
When my heart is overwhelmed,
Keep me dancing on the path
That is higher than I.

May 23

Everyone wanted to come to the airport to meet Jeremy's flight. We were running so late, I wished for a clock with an elastic sweep hand in order to stretch our time.

First, we were hemmed in by slow city buses in the traffic patterns of 82nd Avenue. Red lights caught us in their net at intersections. Pedestrians stopped to look at colored rocks at crosswalks in front of our automobile.

Consulting my watch in the short-term parking lot, I could suspect every lowering jet with landing gear in place to be his.

"We must run!" was my cry to the children.

Having exhorted them in a like voice not to run for years, they galloped forward. My sentence must have cut all their programmed restraints as they began to whoop and laugh entering the terminal. I raced by their side until the blue mat carpet turned to a treadmill speeding in the opposite direction. I thought of the course ahead; this hall to luggage, through the ticketing onto the corridor of the flight gates. From memory I pinpointed a women's room where I could repair the damage to our appearance. I could feel my bangs turn from a well-brushed wall into damp spikes of hair on my forehead. Approaching the luggage area, I increased my speed to my fastest possible sprint knowing I could rest on the escalator up to the ticketing floor. Having passed the children, I shouted, "Come on," without looking over my shoulder.

I didn't see Jeremy standing by his suitcase watching our approach. Once upon him, I was startled and came to an abrupt halt.

He steadied my arm with his hand and smiled. "My flight came in early."

I wanted to laugh at his complete, but simple explanation. Instead, I had to struggle to get my breath. The children, also, could only inhale and exhale deeply at their introduction.

Jeremy took a moment with each one, instead of sweeping his attention over them and back. He repeated Mary Elisabeth's and Anna's name, but with Matthew he shook hands.

Standing at his side, I thought again that Jeremy Foster is a large man. His height would defy all the imaginable extensions ever created in a woman's heel. He was wearing a khaki shirt whose design was parented by the clothing styles of jungle game hunters. Around his neck was a single gold chain.

The feature that I most remembered was his eyes. They were a kind of blue that couldn't be pinned to a sky or a lake for description.

Storing his leather bag in the car, I felt slightly ill at ease. Not knowing what to say, I apologized for the unusually cold weather and dull overcast cloud cover. Jeremy only smiled. I offered my theory for recognizing Oregon from the air: "The land ceases to be visible, and only when the clouds dissolve, a border of California can be traced."

Jeremy wanted to know about the volcano which had erupted five days earlier. He knew the statistics, having watched night and morning news about the big eruption. The mountain was reduced to a flattop, having lost 1,300 feet of peak with an explosion five hundred times the force of the atomic bomb at Hiroshima.

"Mount St. Helens is only forty miles away from Portland. When it finally exploded, I drove with the children to a viewing point. It was a sky filled with cauliflower heads undulating with ash and steam. The winds were blowing north so none of the dust touched the city."

It's never easy for me to drive and talk. Any powers of perception flow into my speech deserting my observations for technical locomotion. I began to cut through company parking lots instead of using the main street. Matthew put his head over the front seat and interjected a command for me to stop. He only gave a one-word explanation: "Bottles!"

I braked sharply as he opened his door and ran to the bushes. He had spotted two empty soda six-packs.

I explained to Jeremy that the state bottle law requires merchants to pay a minimum of a nickel for every can and glass container that is returned.

"It's Matthew's new enterprise. He even takes a wagon to work our neighborhood park."

Matthew interrupted, with specific detail: "I go through the trash cans."

His sentence created an image of an arm risking the perils of old hotdog crusts, and blobs of unused catsup.

I went on to add that the bulk of his business seemed to be in soft liquor packaging. Not having a grocery store in walking distance meant I was enlisted for the final transport of his booty to the market. "I think the back of my station wagon is beginning to smell like secret, wild parties."

Jeremy seemed amused. He even turned in the seat to see the storage room.

"Once the children loaded forty stout malt liquor cans in my car and forgot to tell me. I found them only after opening the hatchback for a pastor and his secretary, having just promised them a devotional book. There, in front of the church office, their pupils seemed to dilate in surprise. I quickly protested that they were not mine, but belonged to my children."

At the curb, I looked up at our house as an observer, not the inhabitant who carries up the grocery bags in thousands of different states of mind. The observer would reflect that the green paint on the siding is a terrible shade, while the inhabitant thinks more of the color it's going to be painted. It's a steep flight of cement stairs up to the burnt-red front porch. The original door knocker from the early 1900s still dominates the entrance. It's a lion with a ring in his mouth. Old Portland houses were built when oil was pennies a gallon. There's a value in the beauty of the window casings being the original natural wood frames. There's a loss in the equally old glass that was installed with enough breathing room to allow an exchange of winter air for our heated interior. Besides our seasonal life in sweaters, I had installed a woodburning stove insert into the living room fireplace.

Jeremy didn't come in and sit down. Neither did he remove his trench coat. Instead, he strode over to the fireplace, and then turned to me.

"Where do you keep the wood supply?" I pointed out the kitchen window to indicate my stack of logs by the refrigerator. He took the ax and wedge to split kindling for a fire. I liked his assertiveness. His activity further destroyed an old prejudice—"Men that sit at desks can't build a quick fire."

Only after the temperature from his blaze began to rise across the room did Jeremy relax. He sat on the floor by the hearth.

He chose that moment to say he had brought me something from Canada. His sentence accompanied the motion of pulling a rectangular box from his jacket pocket. He gave me no time to ponder the idea of a gift itself before he lifted the cardboard lid. On a uniform wedge of cotton was a gold bracelet. The chain looked like close, miniature waves of the sea.

I never had had jewelry. My Timex watch was a single band of practicality. The years of trying to match income to necessities never allowed for bracelets or rings. It was as if I had completely forgotten that hands could be decorated. As Jeremy fastened it himself by opening one link and dropping in the end of the chain, I thanked him.

I turned my wrist watching the gold mesh slide until any slack was filled by my arm. It seemed like a serious moment. I had let myself dream of Jeremy Foster when he was inaccessible, but now with him in my living room, I felt unsure. I intended to keep my heart in an envelope that no gift of jewelry could open.

It didn't matter to the children that we owned a finished basement, separate bedrooms, and a backyard. They wanted to occupy the same eight square feet we shared on the Oriental rug. Matthew abstractedly stroked the hair on Jeremy's forearm.

Studying Jeremy's face, I could tell he was pleased. When the children went outside, he first referred to Matthew by saying, "He likes me." I said nothing, knowing that each one of them loved every man that came to our house.

After dropping Jeremy off at his hotel, I took the Hawthorne Bridge over the Willamette River. In my side vision I could see the transitory reflection of city lights. As I stole glances at the water I thought of the curious mixture of my emotions. In comparing myself with other single mothers, I seemed to desire a marriage relationship more than the rest. The need to love and be loved had long been afloat within me. When there were no men in my life, I cried from the rail for land. Now that Jeremy Foster was beginning to present himself as a shoreline, I didn't know how close to come, and if I docked, what then?

I thought about tomorrow. The children were going to their friend's house.

I could feel any logic breaking down into frivolity. I hoped the sun would come out. I would wear my red silk blouse. I wondered where the decorative haircomb was that a friend had once given me in New York. I wanted to take Jeremy to the rose garden. I would read out loud my favorite prose from the end of the book of Job.

Where were you when the foundations of the earth
were laid? . . .
Upon what are they fastened,
Who laid the cornerstone
When the morning stars sang together,
And all the sons of God shouted for joy?

May 24

It was dark when I woke up. The hour on the clock and the sky were not in agreement. There should have been much more light. After noticing the subdued color of the morning, a slightly acrid smell reminded me of ancient campfire sites.

While the children slept, I phoned Jeremy at the hotel, offering to come and pick him up. None of our

exchange included my first observations of sight and smell.

A gray dust blew across the porch and filled the flower beds. The landscape seemed like the plot of some invisible devil trying to destroy all the colors of the world with ash. A chemical haze covered my windshield. The wipers and small jets of window-washing solvent caused it to darken and streak. My visibility made me imagine that I was driving with venetian blinds.

I am sensitive to suggestion. My appropriate limbs ache when I see people with appendages bound in casts. Medical guidebooks don't enlighten me, but produce like symptoms equaling their description. I was suspicious of my eyes as they began to slightly burn and of the dull throb in my lung cage. Instinctively, I pulled my collar up over my lips and took shallow breaths. There was little traffic on the route to the city center. Whatever cars were in the freeway lanes were driving perceptively slow. I searched my radio dials for an announcer, with an even voice, to read the facts of what I assumed was another volcanic eruption. The radio failed to produce any intelligible sound, while the static simply sounded as if it were trying to clear its throat.

Jeremy was waiting outside under the hotel's green-and-white-striped awning. He was wearing his raincoat. The general public only has clothes for when the sky drops snow or water. It was the first time we saw the horizon filled with uniform spots of ash.

Driving back to the house, I told Jeremy how Mount St. Helens had stood as the single mountain to the north. Its symmetry had made it resemble a child's drawing of a triangle capped in white. I couldn't remember when the news of its first rumblings began.

"I think people were amused at first, as if crackpot scientists were above the timber line hunched over stethoscopes diagnosing a kind of indigestion. Up to the big eruption it was taken lightly, and a cause for jokes: 'Two mountains came into a restaurant, and one had to sit in the smoking section.' "

Habits are a prop of life. Once in the house, Jeremy immediately opened the cast-iron doors and crushed a newspaper into a wad for burning tinder. While he provided the living room heat, I started upstairs to find the portable television to obtain a news bulletin. I could hear the sound of him stirring the grate, arranging the wood. I liked the feeling of him there, an adult mind in the proximity of a living room. The children followed me when I took the celluloid screen out of my closet. If I allowed it, all televised media would call to them, and they would come. It would pipe to them and they would dance. The network news broadcaster had a slide-show backdrop providing one colored picture per topic. Standing in front of a mini-volcano, the anchorman announced the fact of another eruption. The result was an ash plume, composed of pulverized rock, blanketing Portland. The airport was closed. The announcement added that all city residents were advised to remain at home. If automobile use was necessary, vehicles were not to exceed a speed of twenty miles per hour on any road. There would be a minimal number of taxis and buses in operation for public service.

Matthew wondered why it couldn't happen on a

weekday. He took one fist and hit his palm; he already had Saturday off from school.

Anna said, "Now we can't go and see our friends!"

Health warnings were verbally given and simultaneously went across the screen in a typed yellow band: "Inhalation is not recommended for anyone with less than full lung capacity."

The screen filled with enlarged particles of ash. Twenty percent of its composition was ground glass. I started to run my tongue over the roof of my mouth. There was not enough saliva to complete the arc.

I remembered the heavy lead sculptures that were constructed in exact proportion to my lungs. Every day they were placed on a small shelf above my chest as a shield for my radiation treatments. Acting as an umbrella to the X rays, my lungs were still damaged by the scatter.

Before any gloom from thinking about my frailties could ensnare me, the telephone rang. It was Arlene with a short bulletin. She was going to honor the day by rinsing her hair with a new box of prepared coloring, "smoky ash brown."

After wading through disappointment which is the

trough that follows any wave of anticipation, the children recovered with new plans. They were going to study the ash. Matthew asked to go outside and get a box of volcanic fallout from which they could do certain experiments. Wanting to talk with Jeremy, and moved by their quest for science, I agreed by imposing certain conditions. He had to cover his mouth with a scarf and hold his breath while gathering the sample. The children worked in the corner of the room at a maximum distance from the edge of the rug. While asking Jeremy to tell me about his own children, I could see Matthew at the periphery of my vision spooning gray powder into bowls.

Jeremy didn't dig in his wallet for a photo section, but used his own words for description. From the full quiver of having three daughters and two sons, there had been a tragedy of losing the younger boy some years ago. The child was fourteen and visiting relatives in rural Minnesota. The accident was a result of his cousin bringing out a hunting gun for play.

A slight tracing of lines by Jeremy's eyes seemed to deepen as he recalled Justin's accident. The year before, the mother had deserted the family, preferring her own apartment to the responsibility of raising the three remaining children who had not yet married. "I tried reconciliations for years, but she wanted freedoms. Patty finally filed for divorce."

He didn't talk as someone still in pain. There was no change in voice tone, or a kind of quick look that asks me to reply with a sentence from a sympathy card.

"How long ago?" I asked.

"One year," Jeremy replied.

"That's all?" I said, surprised.

It had been my strong feeling to avoid any possible romantic relationship with a recently divorced man. So much of what they did was often a reaction to the phenomenon of being single again.

"Laurel," Jeremy said, while briefly touching my arm. "There were five years of complete separation before that."

It was as if Jeremy knew I had drawn back. I thought that he had a quality of tender sensitivity that could read the slightest nonverbal expression. I stood up, excusing myself to go and get a tray of fruit and bread. I wanted to shake myself from my inclination to ascribe to him every possible virtue.

Jeremy stood up too.

"Let me help you," he said. "Two of us can prepare something twice as fast."

Pausing, I weighed his request, wishing I could stop escalating everything to such an intensity of importance.

"Why don't you slice some of the Tillamook cheese, then," I answered.

As he went out to the refrigerator I made myself think about David Copperfield married to Dora, and his run down the London street crying, "Love is blind."

Jeremy took the tray from my hands to carry it back into the living room. I didn't know Matthew had brought out containers of household condiments. His sister was holding an open peanut butter jar while he was spooning some jelly into a saucer. Then I learned his scientific study was to answer the thesis of two questions. One was an interest in knowing texture, and the other query was what would happen to the ash if it were mixed with household substances. He may have thought he was designing the cover story for *Scientific American,* but all I saw were bowls stiff with concoctions of grit.

As the afternoon faded into evening, the children became increasingly restless. They began to walk around Jeremy, eyeing him as a potential jungle gym. The youngest showed the least restraint. She lay on the floor, raised her hands and feet, and asked, "Do you know how to give a swing ride?"

"That I do," he answered.

I had to intervene before their demands escalated and turned Jeremy Foster into a living amusement park. I didn't want them to begin perceiving the man in the living room as a machinery of thrill rides. Anna asked for the "speedplane." She wanted to ride in circles suspended by her hand and ankle.

As I stopped the children, Jeremy said, "Laurel, I love children. Remember, I had five that were once small." After firmly stating, "Let's do something else," Matthew asked to put on a play. It would be his original version of *Tarzan.* He only requested one freedom for his stage; I would have to let him jump off the couch.

After Jeremy called a taxi to take him back to the hotel, he held both of my hands while thanking me again for the day.

Climbing upstairs, I thought of my heart as a complex labyrinth—but not one without a passage to its center. While gifts of jewelry were genuinely appreciated, and stories of career exploits interesting, neither was the avenue of access. A man had to love Christ, and care about the family as something to be tended.

After brushing my teeth, I wiped off dabs of toothpaste where someone had missed the mark of their bristles. I picked up an assortment of dirty clothes left in a pile by the tub. Leaving the bathroom light on, I turned off the one in the hall.

I considered that my past dating experiences resembled the Greek drama masks of tragedy and comedy. All the leading men had always seen my house as full of extras.

May 25

Even though the rain of glasslike silica had stopped during the night, the ash still held Portland hostage. The morning news outlined the city's clean-up program. The same public vehicles that rescued the main streets from snow would be collecting ash. The bulletin further predicted that the airport would be open by midmorning. Jeremy would now be free to catch his flight.

After breakfast, I knew I needed more horizon when my eyes began tracing mismatching wallpaper seams. In the kitchen I stared only at those potatoes sprouting soft white roots in the vegetable basket. Whenever I feel like walking into the closet and kicking the shoes askew, I know my attitude needs to be taken for a ride.

As I drove down to the city center, I tried to fish for my trouble. I baited myself with questions and cast them into my depths. I know the names of some of the sea monsters that can lurk in a soul. Their mouths are full of teeth, and they wait to feed upon the spirit. Neither *self-pity* nor *bitterness* were out of their cove today. It was a relative to that great carp *resentment* that had been gnawing.

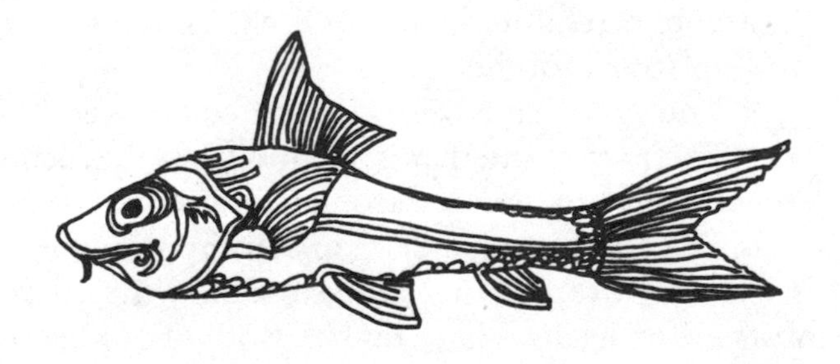

Maybe, I thought, it's my own need that I'm resenting. It propels me to sit by a suitor and listen to a language of colored tissue paper. Fragile and transparent, courtship words are easily folded into fans and flower petals. Having known rejection, I don't want to be led forward only to suffer it again.

I wanted to try and explain it to Jeremy as he seated himself in the hotel dining room. He removed the lid from the coffeepot and regarded me through the steam that rose between us. Watching the vapor rise from his cup in the form of airy acrobats, I held his eye with mine.

"I have an unfortunate history with some of the men that I have known in primary relationships."

I told him about a doctor who had pressed into our family. Our house was his last visit on his way home from the hospital. As we knew him, he refused to draw a border of friendship. When my health collapsed in the Hodgkin's relapse, he knew the poor prognosis of the fourth-stage patient. Yet he persisted in a courtship through the months of chemotherapy. It was two years ago that he had asked me to be his wife. I remember him pulling Matthew up on his lap in the kitchen and asking him if he would like a father.

Within two days of his promise, he called with a statement: "I could handle three children if there were no life-threatening disease, or I could handle the cancer if there were no children; but not both." Jeremy moved his hand up to his forehead.

"You must have been devastated, Laurel."

"The part of me that is vulnerable and trusting was pierced, and now carries around an internal armor and shield. I hear the metal clanking in my thoughts."

Jeremy dropped his hand, touching the edge of his mustache on its descent to his lap. Both of our hands were birdlike, flying up at random during speech.

"Obviously Laurel, I'm finding myself caring deeply for you, but I'm learning in life to be patient with all that is unsolved in my heart."

He continued, saying he was learning to love the questions themselves. He called "questions" those locked rooms or books in foreign print that we are not ready to know, because we cannot live them now.

"The point, Laurel, is to love our questions. Then gradually, without noticing it, we live along some distant day into the answers."

Jeremy pulled the airline envelope out of his pocket and read to himself the time of the departing flight. While he hailed the waiter and played solitaire with his credit cards, I thought I matched his analysis. On the right hand I care deeply, and on the left, have questions. I thought of the "caring" as sheep, and the "questions" as a flock of goats. They were freely roaming over all the indentations of my mind.

Jeremy picked up his Visa card from a plastic tray, and we stood up together.

"I should go to the airport now, Laurel."

While he went to get his luggage I pulled my station wagon up to the front of the Benson Hotel. Watching the door for him, I felt the giant reaper sweeping out to harvest our last minutes. I remembered Jeremy's arrival as a rosy newborn, now doubled up with age.

Jeremy had put on his white raincoat. Opening the hatchback trunk, he lifted up his single leather suitcase. One corner of the luggage pressed against the empty soda bottles.

As we drove to the airport, we noticed that most pedestrians and all employees whose jobs required outside exposure were wearing face masks. I saw one salesman at a corner selling white industrial nose and mouth covers for a dollar. A small elastic band secured them tightly in place. My ride through the streets reminded me of grim future photographs. The captions would read, "Germ Warfare" or "Toxic Air Pollution."

A small circle of land planted in a ring of rhododendrons was the intersection we crossed closest to my house. It is the hub to four directions. A life-size Joan of Arc sat on her metal steed at its center. Someone had tied a face mask across the damsel's cast-iron mouth and another on her horse.

The airport X-ray machine transmitted the contents of Jeremy's briefcase and my purse in sepia tones on the public screen. As we walked through the electronic doorframe, the security guard nodded to us.

We watched the passengers board from the lounge that surrounds the gate. Any that were infirm, blind, or had small children were invited to take their assigned seats first. Blocks of row numbers were called to fill the plane, from back to front. We stood together while every person went into the boarding tunnel. It seemed that our separating was mostly mute, except for his request for me to write him while in England. He gave me a quick hug, and was gone. At the last possible moment for visual contact, Jeremy turned to wave. The gray in his hair seemed luminous in the dark passage.

Walking back along the flight gates, an image of medieval armor prevailed. Entirely buckled, it had a helmet to protect my thoughts, and a breastplate secured against feelings. Yet, back by the car, I knew real courage wouldn't retreat into any self-willed deadening.

I sat at the steering wheel with my ignition key in my lap. I watched the enormous tons of aircraft lift and land. I saw cars creep along the parking aisles looking for a stall. Pedestrians walked by at a crisp pace toward the entrance doors.

I sat there wanting to redesign nature. I wanted just one more handful of mercy to alter humanity. I thought that only those with cupboards of food should feel hungry, not the people with swollen abdomens carrying empty bowls.

I thought loneliness should be the portion of well-matched couples when one is waiting at the corner for the other.

Starting my car, I could answer my own thoughts. I can't push earth closer to the orbit of heaven, and there is a comfort promised to those who mourn. It was a doxology for any who suffer.

May 26

I pulled the ancient and modern suitcases out from their resting place between the washing machine and the wall. Carrying them upstairs in two loads, one in each hand, I thought of how tomorrow we would be folding up the house. Jeremy's visit had marked our last weekend together.

Mary Elisabeth took the blue tin case from me. I could hear her knocking it through the portals of her closet. I predicted she would fill it several times over with select toys to take to her grandparents' house in the San

Francisco Bay area before I intervened with sensible slacks and underwear.

As I put Anna's case by her chest of drawers, I felt the old internal bruise caused by the rubbing of two life-styles. The problem was my belief in the old order. Mothers should be available for every childhood bad dream, wearing aprons with whole-wheat cookies in their pockets. Yet, with some pleasure, I had committed myself to a full schedule in England for the British release of my diary. I didn't even have the excuse of going to earn our support. I had been careful with our burst of income, securing it into interest-yielding certificates. The contradiction gave me fresh pain as I unzipped the case.

I knew the adage of making the time I did have with them a quality experience. All the working mothers I knew could inflate beach balls with that sentence, and toss it around.

As I looked through the pants for those with the least wear at the knees, I tried to dispel my guilt. I did try to take one child with me whenever possible. Also, I knew my work schedule was at its height from the recent publication and would subside within the year. I tried quoting Jeremy Foster over the small piles of garments: "Whenever a parent does too much for their children, the children will not do much for themselves." Yet, I wasn't convinced.

The girls ran from me at the airport to grab seats by the window with an enthusiasm comparable to claiming turkey drumsticks. The special-fare airline provided large white pins for their shirts. Each read "U.M.," unaccompanied minor, in two black capitals. In anticipation of her hour in the air, Mary Elisabeth's last line was concerned with her memory of the in-flight beverage services:

"I'm getting Coke and not milk!"

I was glad for Matthew's company. Bidding good-bye in such a rapid succession of airport visits was taking its toll. I felt like an object that had been whittled. I knew I could bleed and cry easily.

I went into my son's room to inventory his small piles of T-shirts and socks for his backpack. Along the top of his dresser was a lopsided row of plastic sandwich bags filled with volcanic ash. Even as I lifted one to examine his attempt at double packaging, a mist of powder was deposited on the veneer.

I made a quiet statement, "We cannot take this with us."

Matthew had plans for the ash. He thought to sell it in England. He wanted to stand on a street corner and hawk it. He even prepared a slogan for his sales: "One British pound for a Mount St. Helens ounce."

His will was charging mine. It makes the cross in life, when one wants to do what intersects with the will of another. The idea of his rights caused him to slightly raise his voice.

"You are going there to do business with your publisher; why can't I do my business at the same time?"

I refused to argue. His sentence had the tone that baits for a retort. Seeing my "It Is Final" look, he shrugged, and took the ash outside.

Later, after the radiation of his passion had dissolved into half-life, I went to talk to him.

I gave him another form of the endless "appreciation lecture" that parents have, and will give to children.

"I'm taking you to England so we can share some special time together. Later, in the summer, I will take your sisters on a trip also."

In organizing the mail and houseplants for my departure, I remembered a pending doctor's appointment.

I thought of my doctor visits as evenly spaced hurdles that my body had to clear in order to keep my pace. Every six months I was X-rayed and examined for swollen lymph nodes.

I picked up my blue clinic card to look for the phone number of the hospital switchboard. As I turned over my plastic identity card, I remembered all seven digits. They had been branded into my memory. The receptionist's voice from Radiation Therapy accepted my cancellation with an even "Thank you."

It seemed easy to abandon rational, responsible thinking for a lesser level of thought processing. I didn't want to face either the word "remission" or "relapse." I wanted to live for a season as though I had never heard of those things.

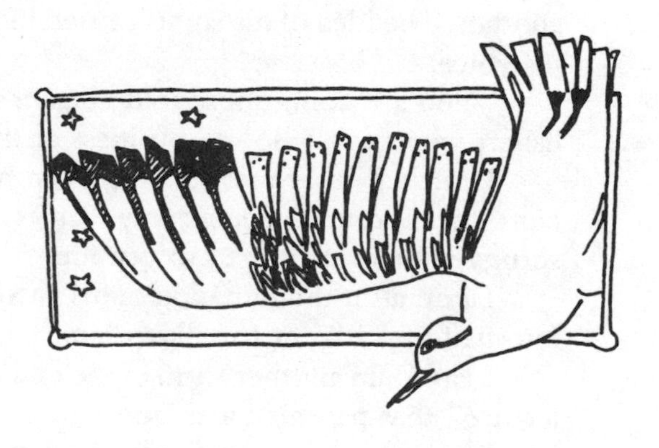

May 28

The biggest bargain flight to Europe has soft edges for the departure date and the return. I only had the freedom of specifying the week, and a computer terminal assigned us the exact day. It would be my responsibility to contact a TWA office in London to know when we could come home. It's an accordion package abroad that can be stretched to almost four weeks or condensed to two by a machine.

Matthew buckled his seat belt and bent over to stow his knapsack. Unzipping a side pocket, he pulled out a portable yellow plastic fan. It fit in his palm like a small flashlight. Activating the battery's energy, he blew his hair up from his ears, then he opened his mouth to cool his tongue.

I regarded his gear with fresh suspicion. Before seeing his fan, I had assumed that all the bulges in the canvas pockets were underwear.

It was going to be a long ride. I anticipated the spots of weariness that would attack my head and spread through my torso, until my whole body would ache in its plea to lie down. It's not my talent to be able to sleep in a chair propped up like a letter "S."

The premonition of pending exhaustion reminded me of a family-history story to tell Matthew. He had been to London once before at Easter time when he was almost a year old. It was the days of cheap charter flights, when planes were outfitted with a maximum number of seats so that passengers' knees brushed the backs of chairs in front of them. We went only because we had never been to Europe. After the flight, we were unable to find any available hotel rooms, forcing us to walk all night searching for accommodations. While British babies were pushed in perambulators built like America's largest luxury cars, Matthew rode in a special backpack. Desperate for sleep, we caught a morning train to a suburban town. Again there were no vacancies due to the public holiday. I went to the police and asked for the list of town residents who had registered to take in boarders. As evening came, we traced out every address only to be turned away. The lady in the last house began to close her door, then remembered a neighbor who occasionally rented rooms. That neighbor made a couch available. . . .

Matthew interrupted my narrative. He wanted to know where we were going to be staying. Shifting from the past to the future, I explained that a man from the publishing house would be meeting us at the airport. He had arranged for us to stay with a family in Rochester. It would only be an hour's train ride to commute to London for our appointments.

To Matthew, questions were like small, empty cups. A little answer filled a cup quickly, and then he began to set up another.

"Tell me about when I was born."

Matthew's tone was hushed. It was his own genesis.

I turned from him and looked out into the dark oval window, wishing I could report on circumstances that were more stable and ordinary.

"Your father and I waited for you."

We had been given a ride to Berkeley when I was six months pregnant, leaving a house on a lake in rural Washington where we had been caretakers. I remembered how we had less than twenty dollars, no car or employment. We lived in a red pup tent on the back of a friend's lot.

"I was so big that Richard would have to push me

up hills and I would arch over my abdomen, swinging my arms in imitation of an elephant."

As Matthew chortled, I remembered how Richard had gotten a job only six weeks before the delivery. We were managers of an old house that rented single rooms with community bathrooms and kitchen facilities.

"Your first bed was a wooden box that your father had built and hung by ropes from the ceiling."

Matthew seemed satisfied by my narration. He wanted to change seats so he could be the first to see the dawn. After I accommodated him, Matthew asked, "Will I ever see Jeremy again?"

I had waited for the children to make some statement acknowledging his visit. They had given no opinion until now. My pause was so lengthy, the child asked me again. I simply stated the truth, that I really didn't know. "He has a lot of summer appointments," I explained. "Maybe your sisters will see Mr. Foster in July when I take them to Los Angeles for my meeting."

Matthew's only reply was, "Lucky!"

The sun set too soon, and was going to rise too early for my body's chemistry. While Matthew dozed, I thought of how I needed this trip to liberate myself from the stimulus of Jeremy Foster. I wanted to live where I wouldn't be perching on every ringing telephone, hoping to hear from him. As I centered my head on the six-inch airplane pillow, I decided that I was putting hinges on the side of my heart so I could open it for a very necessary airing.

London, May 29

When possible, I never check my luggage, but cram my canvas bag under the seat in front of me. Once arriving,

I avoid losing time by waiting at airport conveyor belts. After disembarking in London, we were portable and the first through customs. I knew to look for an Edwin Quibly. Towering above the crowd at the door was a man holding up a sign inscribed with our name. It was written on the kind of cardboard sheet that laundries slip inside packaged dress shirts.

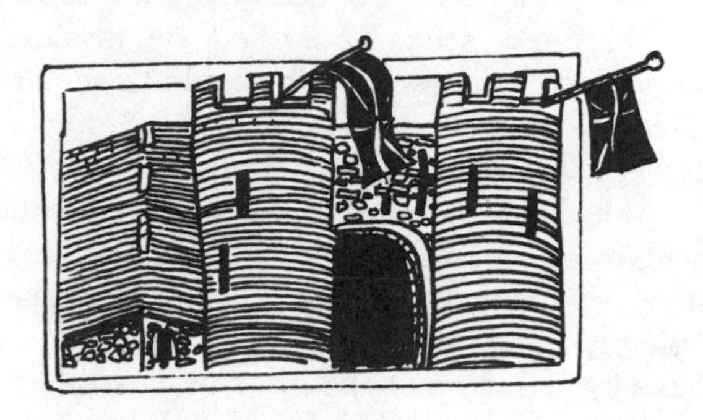

Edwin's height and angular features made him look as if he had an additional joint between his wrist and elbow allowing him extra ninety-degree movements. Even his neck seemed created with a new anatomical moving part between his chin and collarbone. He had dark hair, and his features appeared to have been quickly chiseled. His face didn't have any fineness of small detail, just the essential components for the senses.

After we had settled in his car, my exhaustion created a tunnel in which I felt suspended in a darkness and at some distance from any real communications. Only some British speech idioms broke off from his sentences to reach me. Edwin made regular references to "the dumb-dumbs," some "crumbs," and "Oh, my giddy aunt!"

Seeing Rochester's High Street brought me out of my darkness. I woke up Matthew on the back seat and told him to look out the window.

There was a man strolling in a velvet Prince Albert tailcoat accompanied by a woman in a billowing purple gown. The whole avenue was filled with people in nineteenth-century period clothing. A boy ran by the car in pursuit of an iron hoop held in locomotion by a stick. Seeing his bare feet, short pants, and the square collar of his sailor middy, Matthew declared it was all "weird."

"It's Dickens Days!" said our driver. "Since Charles Dickens lived in Rochester during his childhood and later years, the whole town celebrates its historic resident in an annual three-day program."

Matthew interrupted Edwin's narrative to point out a Punch and Judy show plus an assembly of handbell ringers.

Our driver went on to outline some of the festival's activities that ranged from coach rides to lectures from a museum curator. I agreed to join Edwin Quibly that night to visit a period musical at the Chatham town hall.

Once alone in our room, Matthew took delight that we were living eight hours ahead of his sisters. Settling into bed he wanted to chew the wad of the time change. He felt we had pierced into the future. As he fell asleep, he muttered that we could know all major news events first.

Edwin came to the door wearing a top hat. It made him look like a historical building that had been turned by some enchantment into a man. Over his arm was a red satin frock. Bulging from the skirt's folds was a muslin half slip. It had two seams constructed to hold circular hoops at mid-length and around the hem. Passing me the bundle, Edwin explained he had borrowed them from a friend who works in the costume department at a theater in Kent.

After buttoning the back of my gown, I felt like the kind of gaudy lamp that is won at carnivals by tossing a quarter on a plate.

"I should live on top of a chest of drawers next to cologne bottles," I whispered.

In the car, Edwin handed me a bonnet from the back seat. The hat was a vehicle to support a mass of tiny red feathers which quivered as if charged by an electric current. Edwin addressed my self-consciousness by restating that everyone in Rochester has some kind of costume.

The music hall was at the edge of town where narrow streets beckoned to my every cell curious about old architecture. Having arrived an hour before the performance, I excused myself for a walk.

Turning corners, I exclaimed at quarrystone foundations, and a clock built into an arch. My thoughts began to take the voice of one engaged in conversation. I explained things to a phantom Jeremy as if he were floating by my side with a listening ear. I was beginning to talk regularly to his invisible mind. I wondered if my desire for a relationship had been accentuated by my illness. Sometimes I felt a compulsion to absorb a lifetime into a single hour.

"Jeremy Foster," I thought, "there is in me a haste

to know everything by noon, as I wonder if I'll live to see the evening."

Stopping by a large open gate with gargoyles welded to the top, I concluded that I was simply a time junkie. Entering the churchyard I began to read the multitudes of inscriptions carved in stone. Beside the ancient dates and old poems etched in moss was a freshly dug mound. The largest floral wreath was designed to look like a dartboard created with tightly packed blooms. Propped against the mums was a card that read: "From the boys at the Scarlet Bear Pub."

I didn't see the small crowd that had gathered behind me. As their number grew, the sound of them made me turn. None were in costumes. My recognition of their presence set them free to laugh and call out at the Victorian apparition in the town graveyard.

Instantly I remembered that the night's music program was in Chatham's public hall, not Rochester. I wondered how far I was from the town where people were supposed to be wearing Dickensian dress. I didn't want to explain anything to the spectators because one spoken word would identify me as a dumb American. It became an issue of national pride to keep quiet.

A full hoopskirt is designed for leisure, not speed. Its length and the tension of its expanded circumference kept me from bounding back to the sanctuary of the town hall. As the crowd followed me, I sought comfort in philosophy. I quoted Thoreau's statement on fashion:

> *We all stand like ship-wrecked sailors on a beach and laugh at the old fashions, while religiously following the new. . . .*

June 20

"What are we going to do next?" asked Matthew.

Half the sound of his query was a whine. Even his question was a false wall trying to hide his complaint.

"We have one last commitment with a journalist. You know my work here is to keep these appointments and answer the questions for promoting *Signs of Spring.*"

"That's not work!" Matthew cried.

"It is when you would rather be doing something else."

It was hot and the weariness that had been seeping out of him was being absorbed by me. I scanned the front of a small brick-sided tobacco store for an address. I knew the interview was going to be conducted somewhere on the block. Through the open door I could see a clock advertising Cadbury Chocolates. The script read, "With a cup and a half of milk," and pictured two tipping glasses pouring out a stream of white. The proprietor stood directly under the clock by his cash register.

"We're almost there."

Matthew had stopped at a pay phone to check the coin return. He read out loud some of the instructions for use that were bolted above the dial: "Insert pence only when pay tone (pip-pip-pip) is heard."

My recurring impulse had been to translate Britain into paragraphs to mail on to Jeremy Foster. I had wanted to breathe the old bookstores into letters, and translate into print the view from the top seats of double-decker buses. Having felt that the content of my public communication should equal our commitment, I had trimmed any compulsion into postcards. My few letters to Los Angeles had lacked all passion of description and been limited to small summaries of schedule and appointment.

I had hoped for a certain extinction of my feelings for him in the weeks that separated us from even a phone call. Yet, the thought of him had persisted, a horse that, having once nudged through all my other concerns, never lost its lead.

Taking Matthew by the hand, I pushed open one of the double doors into a narrow foyer. It had a feeling of age. There was a pervading vapor from the year of its construction that couldn't be expelled by paint or new linoleum. Once in the elevator, we could hear the gears grinding their teeth in the basement.

"You know what I'm really mad about," said Matthew. "The whole time I've been here, people have been asking me if I want a biscuit. I say 'no,' thinking it's a round dab of cold bread. Now, I find out the word means cookie."

We sat in the reception area of the offices of a city newspaper. The journalist walked over to us carrying her tape recorder. She had a black patent-leather bow attached to her shirt collar. She unfolded her list of questions. I edged closer to her on the couch.

While she voiced her first query, I thought about one of Matthew's statements. He had seen one diary come and go in publishing, and was now watching the promotion of another. He had made one comment while staring at book jackets in a shop window: "Big deal, the average cat lives a lot longer."

I answered every question while thinking, "This Sunday newspaper story will soon be on the floor of the canary's cage. Low-budget house painters are going to use this edition for a dropcloth." I knew then how much I wanted to go home.

Portland, June 26

In the drive to our house from the airport, my senses could rest in remembering and predicting the familiar configurations of house and store. It was soothing to drive by my church and the neighborhood grocery shop. The products for sale were spelled out in black magnetic letters and hoisted to a billboard by the parking lot. I sang to myself, "Tomato sauce is seven cans for a dollar." It was a stanza to coming home. We called off the street names to Couch, and counted down the houses to our own. A neighborhood dog at the curb was all the committee of welcome Matthew needed.

I had longed for routine, that dancing partner who requires the same steps for each day. As once I had wanted out of its grip, now, I desired to be held tightly.

Ignoring the month's mail that a friend had stacked at my desk bound with a rubber band, I walked through the rooms wanting to savor the knowledge that no one knew we had returned. The month's deposit of dust was of a degree that messages could be traced on furniture surfaces. It seemed to be in excess of what is usual and I wondered if I could suspect the volcano.

It was Matthew who went right to a phone and dialed a friend. After a minimum of dialogue, he asked to go to Eddie's house, enumerating his desires:

Ride a bike,
Throw rocks
Tell stories,
And eat peanut butter and jelly.

I approached the mail as if it were a deck of cards. It could be my game of solitaire to sit and see what the month had dealt. I inverted the pile on my lap and drew the bottom letter. The return address was that of the St. Paul Library Association. I remembered that I was scheduled to be one of their summer speakers at an "Enduring Woman" series. Its contents included a round-trip airplane ticket to their city. Abstractedly, I checked the flight date to find it had elapsed by twenty-four hours. I rushed through the message to find that my scheduled speech had been moved to Friday, June 27. I said, "That's tomorrow," out loud.

It was as if adrenaline vapors rose from the message and were inhaled into my system. All sense of exhaustion was dissolved.

I had to force myself to review the rest of the deck of envelopes. Four letters with a Los Angeles postmark were from Jeremy. I sorted them in my hand by the dates stamped over the postage. I wondered if their contents were going to be hearts or clubs.

Hesitating to open them, I continued to scrutinize the envelopes. All of them had the word "personal" underlined above my address. I knew that was from Jeremy's office culture where a secretary opened all incoming mail unless it was visibly tagged to be private.

I found the contents to be disappointing. He didn't write about dreams or sunrises. Instead, in the first one, he thanked me for the hospitality and added how much he had enjoyed himself during his visit. I could feel his sincerity, yet the formality reminded me of an era that prescribed calling cards left on an oak hall table.

He wrote of office projects, certain goals and ideals. Each letter was signed, "Your loving friend."

I sat musing about their content and my emotions reminded me of furniture that I kept pushing around in my mind. The fact that he had written four times seemed more significant than what he said. While I missed passion or the stringing of language that would show some intensities, I had to admit my own postcards to Jeremy could have been penned by a favorite aunt.

I concluded the matter by noting my own contradictions. Since my feelings lacked stability, I would have drawn away from any expressed fervor on his part to an equal degree that I complained of its lack.

I walked upstairs talking out loud to mock myself in the style of a Barbara Cartland love novel:

"Darling, why didn't you ever tell me of your love?" or, "How can you pledge such affections from your heart when you can hardly know me?"

At least I wrestled with it alone. I felt a sympathy with the mate who endures this nature in a partner. But, I marked, it's the one who suffers the most who sees his own contradictions and can't stop them.

By necessity, I organized an evening flight. While I would be transported to Minnesota, Matthew asked permission to stay with his friend. I phoned my daughters. The voices of the little girls came through the telephone as sweet-scented wild flowers. I yearned to pluck them and pin them to my breast in a corsage of children.

After returning the receiver to the hook, I took one deep breath. I didn't want to go to the Midwest. But I knew it would just be a few more days until we were together.

I decided to telephone Jeremy's office. The secretary sang into the receiver, "Summertree Productions."

When I asked for Mr. Foster, she replied he was out of town. Her voice was three-fourths fact and one-fourth sugar. Wanting to know when he was scheduled back at the office, her answer was, "Next week." She added, "Mr. Foster is in Minneapolis on business."

I asked for his out-of-town number, zipped it into my purse, and packed again.

St. Paul, June 27

I didn't wait long to call Jeremy. As soon as the morning hour reached the breakfast zone, I phoned his hotel.

Letters have certain inherent controls, as there is time to choose a vocabulary that reflects restraint. Telephone conversations are spontaneous, as one mind dials another. Jeremy suggested that he could meet me in my hotel lobby. He added that he had picked up a few things that he wanted to give me. I knew that that probably meant books. Remembering that I had never unpacked some small souvenir gifts brought back for friends, I replied that I also had a present for him.

Pulling the brown bags out of my suitcase, I saw that my collection of European candy bars, bought in a London dime store, had not weathered the trip well. Some of the wrappers were discolored, suggesting that their contents had been melting and solidifying regularly.

In another bag were three old leather-bound books, bought from a junk store's used bin for a few pence. I had forgotten how permeated they were with mildew and other odors of age.

My prize came from Rochester's Saturday flea market. It was a squat, Moroccan leather seat. I thought it might be real camel's skin, and the unraveling stitches in the seams could easily be repaired. I had pulled the stuffing out of it to pack it. Impulsively, I bundled it into the bag with the books and picked up the sack of candy bars to take them all to the lobby.

Once we were together, the length of the separation fell down some hole and was sealed over in the continuity of friendship. His first line seemed to match my last sentence spoken weeks ago as if there had never been any parting.

We went out into a kind of central garden that the hotel was designed around. All of the accommodations on the ground floor had sliding glass doors and patios, while the other guest rooms had a balcony view of the artificial landscape. I was glad the decorators never thought to broadcast recordings of bird songs, or music from a Polynesian fireside.

Jeremy wanted to see what I had brought him. He, himself, was only carrying a briefcase compared to my creased bags. A jumble of scents rose as I placed his gifts on the table. He thanked me once. It sounded like even gratitude that valued everything the same. Yet, I observed he held the books the longest. It made me wish I had more, and could have covered the table with old editions. As Jeremy stacked the candy bars without reading the variety of labels, I restrained my impulse to ask him to unwrap one so I could nibble a chocolate square.

Jeremy opened his case saying, "I thought of you when I saw these things." The lid of his briefcase was designed with an extra sheet of leather creating a pocket. He pulled out five small containers embossed with the label of a Los Angeles antique store. Raising one of the three perfectly square boxes, he revealed a delicate gold pin. Its face was etched in the kind of scrollwork that monks once printed on ancient manuscripts.

Next, he lifted out a bracelet of pearls connected by a single gold chain. Another bracelet followed that was sterling silver on one side and gold plate on the other.

I was wondering how jewelry reminded him of me. I always thought I was best associated with camping equipment.

Jeremy said that the last two boxes were very old rings. The first setting held a single green stone. The last box was introduced as his favorite, six rubies arranged around a single diamond. Both of them must have belonged to women with large fingers as I could shake them off my hand.

Feeling the heat in my cheeks, I knew my face was flushing. It all seemed too rich and excessive. Staring at the open boxes, my emotion turned toward embarrassment. I wanted to sweep into a bush my mildewed books and bars of mottled confections.

Jeremy went on talking as if we had never exchanged anything but a casual slice of toast for a spoon of jam. His sentences had to climb over the wall of my emotional daze. Most of what he said was lost. The contrasts between our offerings to each other looked like the opposite ends of the earth. Mine was dark, steamy, and "third world" while the white boxes with cotton were a polar ice cap. My humiliation blocked most of what he said. Finally, a line about the size of his brother's hands compelled me to pay attention.

"Much of my family lives four hours from here, due north."

Before parting, I agreed to drive with him the next day for a short visit. Leaving early, we could return in time for my Portland flight which would connect with the girls who were to be routed home.

After speaking to the library association, I was finally alone. Certain fears piped to me. Taking the jewelry out of all the boxes, I laid the pieces across the surface of the hotel room table. It cannot work, I thought, our cultures are just too different for any relationship more than friends.

I thought of us in a kind of multiplication table of opposites:

> My state park campsites equaled in number
> his double-bed hotel suites.
> It was one old station wagon
> against one shining
> Mercedes-Benz.
> For every flannel shirt I wore,
> he had twenty with designer labels.

Deciding to back away from any more commitment, I raged at the pain of all the couples who never quite matched.

I found it appalling that my admiration had jumped to love and from love to even questioning matrimony, in a moment.

The pillows on the bed were stuffed with feathers, instead of the standard particles of foam. With my fist, I could beat out a hollow for my face. My words were muffled in such a close range of bedding.

"Our essential values seem the same. Culture is the

problem. You, Jeremy, need a woman with fat fingers to wear all the rings."

Exhaustion must let insanity crawl along its edge. A craziness had seemed to creep between reality and my thoughts.

I cried at the idea of women with fat fingers that are greasy with materialism. They err in evaluating men by what they can give them.

"Repent," I said, and fell asleep.

June 28

I never knew Jeremy could sing. He lifted up verse after whimsical verse about a group of Irish musicians. His voice boomed between the windshield and the back window about McNamara's Band. The chorus extolled their performance at wakes and weddings.

If our hours in the car were a tablecloth, he spread it with light dishes of childhood stories and music. After my cares of last night, I felt it wasn't the right time to spill things and make dark blotches.

The apartment that his mother lived in was a part of eight connecting ground-floor units. It looked like a small rural motel surrounded by long solitary fields.

Mae Foster walked out to the car. She didn't waste any minutes on a formality of waiting for company to knock. The upturned corners of his mother's face held a number of connecting indentations which supported ample cheeks. Mrs. Foster brought us through the door intending to escort us to a chrome and formica table set for lunch.

I didn't want to go past the baskets of quilt scraps. Treasures of stitched colored cottons were tucked in the few feet between the couch and her kitchen. Mae talked old sewing lore. Tapping her head, she said, "It was those who were not quite right that were first given crazy quilts to make. That pattern of irregular scraps sewed together was for the women who couldn't be trusted with scissors."

The chief decoration on the walls, and the object that covered any flat furniture surface, were family photographs. Years of time could be traced from the black-and-white shots of fedoras to the slick colors of the great-grandchildren's school pictures. Plaques of Bible verses were sprinkled like grains of salt among the images of the extended family.

I looked around noting the clutter of small ceramic pieces, including Japanese dolls whose heads were attached to their body by a spring, vibrating on the shelf.

In the center of the table was an island of condiments. Besides the seasonings in their shakers, there was catsup and peanut butter. Those bottles and jar of spreads were never moved, only replaced when consumed.

The boy resident within Jeremy began to spoon through his mother's bowl of homemade noodles looking for those that had clumped together while cooking in the steaming broth.

I refused coffee, so Mrs. Foster served me Kool-Aid as an alternate beverage. Knowing the ingredients were exclusively water with sugar, plus a chemical fruit flavoring, I still drank it. That which has been swallowed for the sake of good manners cannot be numbered. Before I could protest, Mae filled my cup with more bright green fluid. Most homes operate by one of two mealtime philosophies. The offense will either be "wasting food," by leaving uneaten portions, or "gluttony," eating what you neither need nor want. Instinctively I knew we should clean our plates. Behind my seat was a rhododendron whose potting soil absorbed my drink.

Mae Foster's antenna for hospitality was soon quivering over my empty cup. Pursuing me with the pitcher, she quoted the need for more liquids in the summer. My thirst had become an issue of health. On the grounds of my well-being, Mae overrode my refusal. Only while clearing the table was I able to pour the residue down the sink.

Once sealed in the quiet of the car, I turned to Jeremy and exclaimed that he had never told me he was reared in a pioneer farming family.

"At one time we lived in a house constructed of roughly hewn logs, and I can remember feeling lucky when we got orange crates to put our clothes in."

Out of the window I saw acres of corn. The speed of our vehicle made the cultivated rows have the moving perspective of wagon spokes. The air smelled as if it were filtered through the fields.

"Jeremy, I left the suburbs where I grew up sure of one fact. I didn't want to devote my life to building a pyramid of things as a memorial to merchants' ads. Then, I found the university to be mere stockpiles of knowledge with diplomas stuck as flags at the top. I wanted wisdom, and thought it would be better obtained in watching a garden grow. That's when I married a man who promised to homestead in Alaska with me.

"Jeremy—" My voice got exuberant.

"I see those same values in your mother, which helps dissolve some fears I've had about our relationship. Frankly, you are just 'down-home folks,' even wearing those designer initialed socks." I pointed at the floorboards. "And owning your Dyco oil stocks." My arms swept up.

Jeremy laughed and turned his face from the road to lock his gaze momentarily with mine.

"These are my priorities, Laurel. It's the worship of God first, the care of one's family second, and last is one's work."

It sounded as old-fashioned as the orator invited to speak to the farmers at the grange hall. But it was exactly what I needed. For the first time I felt the freedom to fasten around my arm one of the new bracelets he had given me.

Portland, July 1

The little girls' voices found passage through the neighbor's rosebush, and over to me and Melanie sitting on the top step of the porch. Because of the time of day, there was no shadow, except directly under our knees. Melanie leaned forward to rest her chin on her hand. There were a few flecks of steel-blue paint on the blunt ends of her hair. She was going to watch the children while I went for my medical check-up.

"It is hope and dread," she said.

I agreed with a look.

When we were in Minnesota I had tried to tell Jeremy the survival-rate statistics for a fourth-stage pa-

tient. He cut through my paragraph saying, "I know you are well."

Melanie was quiet. Her silence was eloquent. She was cautioning me now, for Jeremy's sake.

"He's never even been sick," I said.

In my pause I reflected how this worked against his understanding the flash floods of some diseases.

She said, "Explain relapse to him again."

"I'm taking the girls with me to Los Angeles in about a week and a half."

"Laurel, you can't wait that long."

The difficulty of our subject was stripping the edges of our sentences to a few key words. We both nodded with whole paragraphs sealed between the exchange of our eyes.

Taking the back roads to the medical school, I found myself driving under the speed limit, and cheering for any traffic light that would suspend forward motion. I was enticed by store window displays. Even motor parts shops and a warehouse of plumbing supplies seemed more interesting than visiting the doctor.

I thought to dispel my anxiety by addressing my body.

"After all the whole-grain wheat I have fed you and the vistas of hiking trails you've been exposed to, you went ahead anyway and got mixed up with cancer."

It played through my mind as a grim cartoon. Animated hoodlum cells had first started loitering around my lung. The gang warfare began. The name of the specific cancer cell of the Hodgkin's lymphoma is "Reed Sternberg." I saw it abbreviated "R.S." and etched in cellular black leather jackets above a skull and crossbones.

Once at the hospital, the crowding of the public parking lots gave me my last free minutes before entering the institution. After giving my name at the receptionist's window, I was immediately escorted down the hall to an examination room.

I was wondering on what wing of the hospital did the floor-maintenance janitor pour out the largest dosages of disinfectant. Maybe he felt it was too late if one had cancer, and gave this strip of linoleum the minimum.

When it was Dr. Moss that opened the door, I could feel a wave of confidence. As the chief of staff of the radiation department, he had managed my case through both sieges of the disease. He first looked for swollen lymph nodes by squeezing my neck and armpits in his search for the stiff black jackets denoting gang activity. He couldn't find any unusual loitering. The doctor sent me to the X-ray department with a coupon requesting pictures of my lungs and spine. He paused at the door.

"I'll call if there is any abnormality, Laurel."

That evening I phoned Jeremy. Even before picking up the receiver, I recited the facts from medical journals. While dialing the Los Angeles area code, I repeated one of Dr. Moss's observations. I would refuse to be charmed into some conversational galaxy. I plunged to the fact.

"Jeremy, I have spent time with the families of many

cancer patients. Often, I find a defense against reality is in their denial of the disease."

I detailed the doctor's warning that my whole skeletal structure was prematurely aged and damaged from the aggressive treatments. I quoted for him the possible brevity of remission.

"It was a senior staff member that told me that it's a twenty percent chance of only a five-year survival."

He wouldn't be sober. He even laughed while saying, "Benjamin Franklin wrote, 'God does the healing, and the doctor collects the fee.' "

July 11

The telephone is today's instant letter. While my senses were being poured into the phone receiver, Matthew stood at the door in his pajamas whispering if he could make his sisters a small snack.

I came down the stairs to find all the kitchen counter space dissolved in his preparation of a sweet dough. I caught him trying to convert his concoction into the texture of cookies by frying his thin cakes in my skillet.

Anna had carved "J.F." into one with a butter knife. Holding it up in her palm, she asked what time was our flight to Los Angeles. I told her late afternoon while watching the angle of her hand continue to invert, tempting gravity.

"Since Mary and I are coming with you, I'm taking this to Jeremy Foster myself!"

While Matthew confirmed that he had his things packed to go to his friends', Anna's confection slid to the floor. Undaunted, she washed it and put it in a plastic sandwich sack for its transit to the south.

Once we had landed at Los Angeles International my eye scanned the terminal windows. I knew Jeremy was there and my desire to see him seemed strong enough to draw his face up to press the very glass. The stewardess interrupted my intensity by coming with her pencil to make a notation of Mary Elisabeth's seat number. She explained that the maintenance crew would replace the bottom cushion with a dry one before the flight continued to Phoenix.

I was impatient with the passengers who blocked the aisles while checking the overhead luggage bins. There was enough space between their heads and the roof of the plane that I wished I could levitate above the crowd, and fly to the exit. Instead I emerged from the back with the two girls, who were both wearing free plastic flight wings.

Jeremy was waiting for us. He stood at a distance from the door. His face had tanned since I had last seen him in Minnesota. After hugging Anna, he picked up Mary Elisabeth, then stiffened and set her down quickly. Her wet dress made a number of dark splotches on his blue cotton shirt.

It was my turn to be greeted. The welcome wasn't felt in his brief flying kiss, or his movement to take our bags. Jeremy used an ordinary salutation, but I sensed his affection as the living current in each gesture.

At the car door Anna spilled some of her red stirring sticks onto the asphalt. She had gleaned them along with bags of peanuts from the aisle. I could only guess at the number of snacks she might have consumed. While watching her climb into the back of the Mercedes, my pervading thought was a hope that she wouldn't become carsick.

Jeremy mentioned Mount St. Helens. He explained that the evening news had carried a bulletin about the buildup of another pressure layer that would release a volume of ash and steam into the atmosphere. I wondered if the smog at our horizon was prompting Jeremy to talk about the weather. It was diffusing the blue into a dark line.

I told Jeremy about my local grocery store printing "Volcano Alert" onto their paper sacks. Stamped in red was a list of safety precautions which included the necessity of extra food storage for the days of being shut inside by an eruption.

"Stores are now stocking souvenir ashtrays, constructed with a layer of volcanic dust encased in glass. I almost bought a pen with a gravity chamber that shakes the ash into fresh turbulence as one writes."

While he laughed I could feel my emotions rising. I didn't want to talk about egg timers utilizing Mount St. Helens fallout. I wanted to tell Jeremy my feelings. It would be a simple declaration of me being comfortable next to him.

I spoke in a quiet voice.

"Jeremy, I was just thinking about us as two chairs pushed together. Our styles are different but our upholstery seems to match."

We pulled up the circular driveway to the hotel where I had reservations from the women's fellowship that had scheduled us to come south. The children saw the room as only a passage to the swimming pool. To me, our hotel room smelled as if the air in it was not a free commodity, but one provided by the hotel at a consumer cost. As I inhaled, it was as if the air for breathing was rationed to be used innumerable times before being discarded for any that is fresh.

Alone for a few minutes, I tried not to rush while changing my blouse for one with shorter sleeves. Wanting to calm myself, I slowly pushed the buttons through the fabric openings and straightened it in the mirror. It was my white shirt that I had spent a winter embroidering with birds on vines. One wing took days to color with thread. My feelings seemed too high. It was as if ecstasy was on a trapeze. I couldn't bring it down, but I could stop it from swinging wildly within me.

Jeremy was waiting out at the pool in the central plaza. I didn't need sight to find its edge. The heat baked together chlorine vapors and perfumed tanning oils. The majority expression of the patio inhabitants was the pose and look of deck chair apathy. I pulled over a Mexican tooled-leather seat by Jeremy. I put my chair on the side of him that offered shade from a eucalyptus tree. There was no hurry for speech, just a certain camaraderie of sitting together on a hot afternoon. Jeremy broke the silence with a voice that was quieter than usual. He spoke of loneliness, that emotion of isolation, as if it were a separate ball in space.

"I've always had my work."

With almost a drawl Jeremy seemed to suggest that one's labors can keep it in orbit and at a distance.

"But now, the depth of our dialogues just exposes the pain of not sharing things together to a greater degree."

His statements required no response from me. To

talk, even in agreement, would only subtract from the empathy of the moment.

"Laurel, we really know a communion that seems to add a new significance and dignity to everyday life."

Somewhere the children were jumping onto the pool's stairs, a gardener was watering flowering plants in large clay pots, and people were adjusting their bodies to catch the rays of heat. But it all seemed very far away, and hardly in the focus of periphery vision.

Jeremy leaned toward me. He said quietly that he wanted me to be his wife.

I felt a physical impact from his words as if he had unexpectedly thrown a solid object at me. I was immediately out of breath and my face flushed. The question seemed too large for me to catch or hold. The exertion lay in my own longing for intimacy buffeting against my sense of careful prudence.

When I looked at Jeremy I could tell he was only feeling my caution as a reply. His face reflected the extra brightness of someone near tears. Within a moment, that wave of moist luster seemed to roll back within his being.

In the deepest part of me I cast the whole question of matrimony up into the courts of God, beyond time and reason, for an answer.

And to Jeremy I quietly replied, "I don't know this yet," while putting my hand on top of his.

July 12

I couldn't sleep. Maybe the folds in my brain that cross its surface like riverbeds had moistened with rest, but they never knew the real tides of sleep. I couldn't let go of the solemnity of Jeremy's request, along with certain memories.

At age twenty-nine, I had filled jars with strawberry jam, iced them with sealing wax, and thought I would always be married to Richard. I assumed I would grow old in his kitchen, and my last act in life would be to fold my apron into the triangle of a retiring American flag. By the following summer I knew routines were not a reliable tool for prediction. I wondered if all I had lived through was to prepare me for marriage or warn me against it.

I was glad for morning and its duties, but I found my mind could never quite stand at full attention. The hostess for the luncheon came for us at the hotel desk. While she explained that the women at the head table were to eat first, I found myself wishing for her simplicity. She was a large woman whose skin reminded me of a kind of transparent paper folded every May into Mother's Day cards. Instinctively, I knew that her wallet strap had to be bulging over a number of grandchildren's photos. Once in her car, she continued to detail all aspects of food servicing. I wanted life to be as simple as the ordering of cheese slices on a serving platter.

I didn't feel genuine using my prepared speech. Instead, my inclination was to talk about Jeremy Foster. I wanted to present him and our relationship as the body of my address. After a question-and-answer period, everyone should write on their napkins whether I should marry him or not. I would want to gauge the intensity of their decisions by suggesting that those adamant against a union ring their glass with a knife, and that those for us lift a spoon of rich pudding in a salute while I tallied the vote. I could begin a search for wisdom in this multitude of counselors.

Instead, I refrained from hijacking the microphone and stayed to my course of regular paragraphs.

It was a sea of women. The raised platform let me see their laps as well as their faces. As I gave detail to my last pregnancy and birth, I thought how civilization had taken away our town well where we could meet with clay jars at the noon hour. So now, one place to exchange admonition and comfort is the luncheon.

On the flight back to Portland, I knew that my heart's impulse was to say "yes," and make a commitment. I wanted to sign the name "Laurel Lee Foster" on an airplane napkin above the script that read, "Fly the friendly skies, United . . ."

But I knew that my heart wasn't entirely reliable as an instrument for guidance. *Wisdom is the principal thing.*

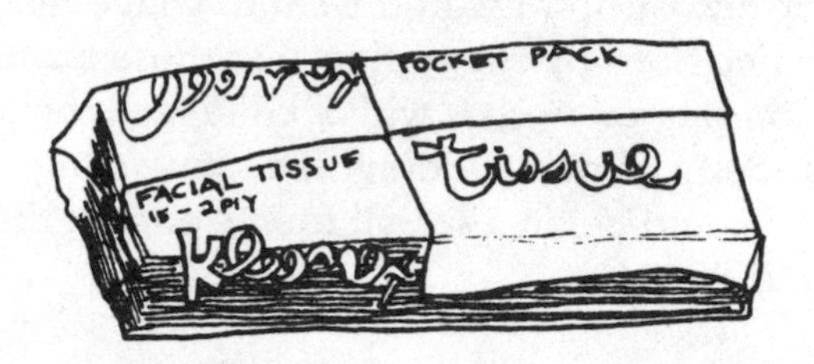

Portland, July 15

A dewy gathering below Mary Elisabeth's nose was my first clue that some influenza had claimed a victim. I blamed swimming pools and air conditioners as the incubator of the newborn cold. I bought the child her own miniature package of Kleenex to substitute for her shirt sleeve. My purchase saved us from listening to unnatural suction noises. I hoped glasses of orange juice would be the elixir for Mary Elisabeth's restoration.

After lecturing Anna to avoid using her sister's drinking glass or toothbrush, I, in turn, tried to dodge some of the close-range confidences that the four-year-old child believes are proper conversational distances.

Even with precautions, my throat became scratchy. It escalated to where every swallow seemed to meet the resistance of an ever-enlarging grade of sandpaper. My speech became an imitation of old doors at odds with their hinges. My cough lacked a certain conviction because it gave no release. My physical decline exceeded Mary Elisabeth's experience with the influenza. She never curtailed any activities, while I lived between the bed and the couch.

"Is it Hodgkin's disease?"

Matthew stood over me. There was no inflection to his question. He had the same tone that one uses to inquire about the weather when devoid of true curiosity. Having walked into the living room from the kitchen, he rotated a carrot between his thumb and finger.

"Go to the doctor. He may want to do an autopsy."

"Biopsy," I said, raising my voice. "And they don't do it for flu."

Night brought fevers. I felt suspended on the two sides of the moon, where life can't be maintained either in its heat or in the chill of the side in shadow.

My dreams were brief and brightly colored. Old classmates were loosed from my memory and saluted me in the corridors of sleep. I asked each one if they would like to see my wedding pictures. I pulled out a narrow strip of four connecting shots. It was the kind of photography done by a machine in a dime store booth. The camera is activated by two quarters deposited after the subject has isolated himself in front of a small screen.

Both Jeremy's and my face were crowding the frame. Our features were distorted in four different views of comic proportions.

July 16

A healthy body doesn't seem to exist. It just responds to the ignition panel to move at command. I tested my machinery by first probing it with the thought of how I felt, then testing its performance going down the stairs. I was under the speed limit, but in operation. As a cancer patient in remission, I was comforted that it had only lasted days and not months. But all illnesses have their common discomforts.

I met Matthew in the kitchen. He was searching the cupboards for appealing food products. Since the back door was open, I knew he had completed his analysis of the refrigerator. I found him kneeling on the counter going through the grocery boxes on the top shelf.

I thought that the species of the ten-year-old boy now covers all the inhabitable continents. Relentlessly driven to consume his own body weight, the boy is on an endless forage for provisions.

Matthew turned around at my entrance to sit on the counter. While resting one bare heel on the drawer knob, his other foot massaged mosquito bites at his ankle. He listed boxes of packaged cereals he wanted me to purchase. In a mood to counsel, he recommended I increase my measures of discipline with his sisters.

"Jeremy Foster has asked you to marry him, hasn't he?"

The name was uttered by stringing together the given name and family name into one sound. I knew his ear must have been around the corner from one of my phone conversations when I had been asking for advice. Giving him a shrug, I indicated by look and gesture that the subject was behind high walls.

Matthew didn't recognize that I had refused him entrance to the issue. He continued in a rambling sort of voice, "If you don't marry him you'll make the mistake of your life."

I looked at him closely. The child was wearing two contrasting pajama pieces. His bottoms were imprinted with football players on flannel, while his shirt extolled the American space program. I put my hands on his shoulders, wanting to squeeze comfort down his arms and across his heart.

Leaving him, I walked out the back door to sit on the side of the step that was in the sun. The light filtering through the leaves undulated in and out of shadow. It gave the illusion that the yard was a shallow reflecting pool.

In memory, I inventoried my phone conversations, wondering which one or part Matthew had heard. My parents had been hearty in their endorsement. Jeremy had flown to Fremont, taken them to dinner, and written a thank-you note which Mother had read to me over the phone.

Melanie had pointed out our cultural differences as a potential conflict.

"Looking at your backgrounds, I wouldn't be surprised if he slept at night in an old suit and tie, while you probably wear a Kelty backpack."

Arlene wanted me to be happy, but advised me to go ahead only when I was absolutely sure.

It seemed to me that once I had received the proposal, I was living constantly with the configuration of a possible marriage. I was rising with it every morning, and the phantom of saying "yes" or refusing was riding heavily upon my consciousness. I thought vehemently that this creature of my indecision has a long silk cape. On one side are hopes, which invert at random to fears. And even a definite answer to Jeremy won't completely vanquish it.

It's what I didn't know about Jeremy that constituted the risk. I thought of how every person is built with certain fault lines, crevices within their character. Some they know about, while other finer cracks lie hidden, not well defined, yet with that separation between what they should do and what they don't. It was Jeremy's twenty-year life-style that I pondered. Stick by stick, I laid out the kindling that time could ignite into resentment.

I questioned him once if in the past he had chosen in his priorities the nurture of his business over that of his family. The memory of his answer to this charge took its turn for a defense.

We had been sitting in a restaurant. All detail of line

and menu had faded, but his answer blazed in a confession that he was often absent because of his projects.

"I know now that it was a mistake, Laurel."

He didn't dodge my bullet with any shield of excuses, or hide from it behind the boulder of a miserable homelife.

His voice led me back three thousand or so years to ancient days. He called forth Old Testament nomads and quoted their priority of labors in taking a new land. First they piled up rocks to build an altar, erected their tents, and then dug a well.

"This," Jeremy explained, "is the order of putting the worship of God first, then the care for the family, and last the business of giving the neighborhood its drink.

"I have learned an obedience to this principle by what I've suffered."

Then the picture in my mind changed to Jeremy turning to me from his steering wheel. We had been driving in the Los Angeles hills, and my eyes left the low scrub bushes to look back at him.

"I would want to adopt your children. Give me the gift of a second chance."

Matthew slammed the back door, having followed me outside after cooking some toast for himself. Distinct crumbs clung to his flannels.

"You like him, don't you?"

I nodded, deciding against a brief speech on how we shared the same values and common goals.

I took a piece of Matthew's bread wondering where the line was: "A little child should lead them."

July 26

From the twelve available decorator colors for Bell telephones, I had chosen forest green. Now, one year after the installation, the cord came out of the receiver with a number of sagging loops as a result of being stretched beyond its power of elasticity. A subtle grime surrounded the three digits that were the first numbers for local calls.

I pulled the phone into my room and shut the door. The function of the bedroom walls was just to enclose me in a private booth so I could ring Los Angeles.

Jeremy first answered with the hasty monotone of a businessman. Once identifying the caller, his voice began to hold life: seed, bud, and fruit in one "Hello, Laurel."

Having once proposed, Jeremy never repeated the direct question of marriage. I brought up the subject. I asked him about something he had once said, although it was never spoken in the context of our relationship:

"Speak to me about your certainties, I have enough uncertainties of my own."

His response was to declare a commitment to me that encompassed his whole spirit.

"I would not leave you or forsake you, Laurel."

Confident of my direction, I gave my answer.

"Yes, I will be your wife."

There was no going back, no inching away from a line that was clear and drawn. Our bits of talk settled into the practical. Jeremy asked me to open my calendar to see if we could establish a prospective date. He closed in on October 20 as I had not scheduled any commitments for a space around my birthday.

The date gave us a three-month pivot point for organization. Jeremy said he would have to find us a house in Los Angeles. I, in turn, would organize a wedding and prepare to transport all of our things to the south at that time.

I found the two girls in the living room. They had taken a blanket and tucked it into the back crease of the couch. The opposite end was draped over two wooden chairs and secured on the seat with books. I crawled under the construction to share the news. Anna and Mary Elisabeth were animating two stuffed animals. Both girls' hands were encircling a plush, synthetic fur back. The creatures were being jerked in short hops on the rug. Before I could talk, Anna explained that this canopy was a house and their two bears were husband and wife.

Getting up in the night, I could find only pens with ink chambers dehydrated from age or lost caps. My journal lay open, and an image, like a bird, had landed on me. But it could only flutter in my mind while I searched for some tool for recording. I finally chose a Crayola from a box on Anna's shelf. The color gray was an unpopular shade, and had enough point to print:

For days I rolled with the question of what to do.
It was if I were compelled
To stay at sea
Until I found the solid continent of my answer.
Stung by the spray of my own thoughts,
Tossed by the wind of other opinions,
I held fast to the wheel of desiring truth.
Once I was willing to throw
Whatever was asked of me overboard,
I saw the shore line;
It was his cry for a second chance.

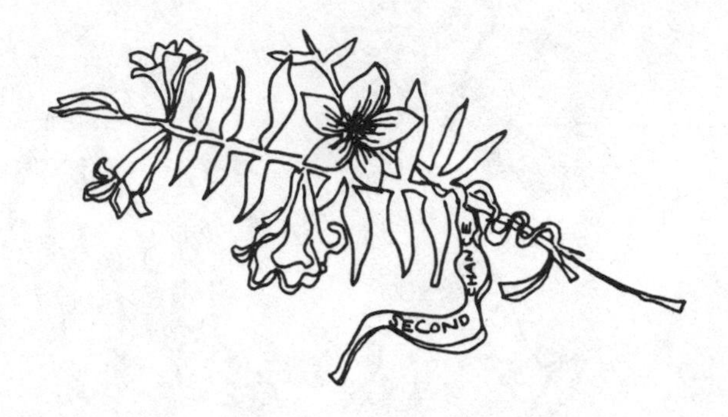

August 10

There's a mystery to a bed. My mattress has a given number of coils and tufts of foam. Yet its comfort is not tied to its construction, but to the hour, and exhaustion. I couldn't sleep. I tried two methods for reinducing slumber. I refused the impulse to keep readjusting my body, and neither would I look up to check the time. Instead of thinking of a number of things, I tried to hold to one thought, hoping that it would lead me back into that state void of meditation. Nothing worked. I snapped on my light and looked at my watch. It was near dawn.

I kept thinking about the American wedding. The traditional style reminded me of a senior prom where the bride is the head of the decorating committee. The idea of having a predetermined color or two as a theme in the ceremony amused me. It becomes the law of the hour that everything match. The bridesmaid's shoe has the same hue as the carnation pinned to the usher's chest.

There were the rental stores which fill their display rooms with wedding props: bridges and arbors for backdrop, and a pair of animated doves whose beaks could drip punch into a guest's cup.

On the other hand, I didn't want to write every aspect of the service: "After composing all of our own music, Jeremy built the instruments himself, while I was using my hand loom to weave the reception napkins."

I appreciated the new freedoms allowing for one's own expression of location and costume to surround the exchange of vows.

"Dearly beloved, we are gathered here today to witness this union in a cornfield, and there will be a potluck and hoedown afterward."

Once I saw a bride's dog led down a church aisle on the arm of the maid of honor.

Out of my window the shade of the sky clearly showed where a compass needle should point to the east. I thought it's hard to believe that the night moves as quickly as the dawn. There was no northwest cloud cover to offer resistance to a summer morning.

Mary Elisabeth pushed open my bedroom door. One side of her head still had a form of braid, although every short end stood out from it until it resembled a kind of feather from the number of loose hairs. Once invited in, she took possession of the pillow and a luxurious helping of the mattress.

I condensed the thought that a couple can design their own wedding. That was enough stimulus for Mary Elisabeth to begin her own free association for the ideal ceremony. She envisioned an enormous hand-painted box up on the altar. It would have to be big enough, she explained, so everyone in the church could see it.

"There's little velvet curtains that should open for a real puppet show."

Apparently some puppet with a large mouth would lead us in our pledge of union.

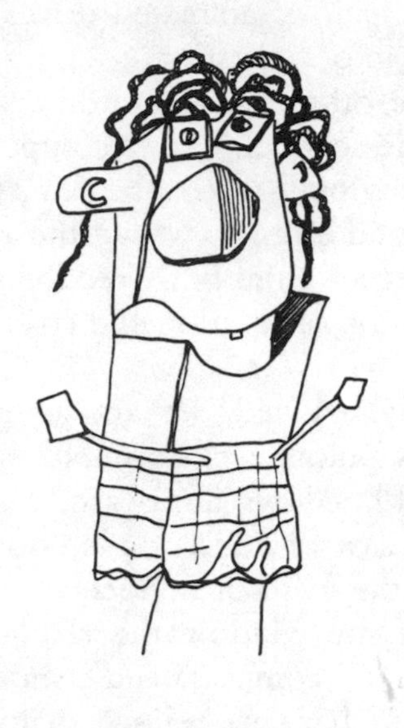

Hi, yah,
Hi yah, Jeremy.
Where's your left side?
That's the lady.
Are you ready
For better or worse?
Cross your heart
And hope to die
If your promise
Is a lie. . . .

At the conclusion a hand puppet named Cookie Monster would be introduced. She described him as being covered with bright green fur and having the job of inviting everyone to the reception.

"What would you serve?" I asked.

"Cokes and peanuts just like on the airlines, with a big chocolate cake."

"It would be a memorable service," I agreed.

Switching ears with the telephone receiver, I released one side of my head from the warmth of listening.

I interrupted Arlene with my own news.

"Jeremy's coming to visit. He is wringing his schedule to squeeze out of it a day in Portland."

He was the only man I knew who subscribed to the *North American Flight Guide* in his monthly load of magazines. It detailed the flight schedule of every commercial airline carrier.

Arlene then asked what my wedding with Richard had been like. I needed to pause while pulling out such a faded photograph from my memory.

"The two of us walked to church together with my dress wrapped in tissue paper in a backpack."

I remember we had talked about tree roots, and wondered how they looked and the extent of them under the earth.

"After walking down the church aisle the pastor first redirected how we were standing by inverting our positions in front of him before speaking any solemn word.

"Then during a pastorly exhortation for keeping humor as part of the marriage, Richard started swaying at my side. He didn't faint until after the vows were said and we were walking out.

"He collapsed on the bench of an empty pew a little more than halfway between the altar and the back doors."

Neither Arlene nor I laughed. Maybe we were each waiting for the other to make a sound which the other would match. But we both remained silent.

"That week I had just turned twenty-one," I said, thus trying to cast my story back into the lake of youth.

The memory didn't sink as I said good-bye, but floated under the surface. It was like bubbles of recollection.

Newly married, we had framed a miniature cabin on

the back of a truck to take to Alaska for homesteading. With water tanks under the rafters and a wood stove, we had pulled out of Portland.

It was in that mobile house that I read the Sermon on the Mount, and first began to learn about Jesus.

August 15

Every morning has its own voice. Sometimes it's a sergeant barking the day's orders. There are times it's contemplative with a tone that's neither leisure nor haste. But with Jeremy in town, the early light seemed like the voice of a friend calling outside my window:

"Laurel, Laurel, we've got bikes to ride, forts to build."

Walking downstairs, I anticipated all the things I wanted to show Jeremy. The contents of my house are arranged in commemoration of neighborhood garage sales and secondhand shops. It was Jeremy's countersuggestion over the phone that we take the children to the Oregon coast.

Since Portland is a small city, the pine-tree covered hills are always visible marking its metropolitan borders. To the east Mount Hood stands in snowcapped prominence among the peaks of the Cascade Range. Jeremy's hotel was west, along the route to the ocean. He jumped into the front seat wearing shorts, white tennis shoes, and the kind of athletic socks that have two bands of color at the top.

"News," he said. "I have found the right home."

I marked that he had wanted to tell me in person.

Jeremy described a small area of mountains that back up to Malibu, called Topanga Canyon. Within the Los Angeles sprawl, it's a pocket of horse farming and residential acreage. He defined the house as a Spanish adobe with a tile roof. Jeremy's descriptive language and real estate fact sheet reminded me of the glossy full-page photos of interiors that compose advertising layouts in women's magazines. The bottom line talks about some new chemical shine in a spray bottle. For a moment I felt gratitude that the sky had opened and everything I had ever wanted was falling to earth. I imagined my name inscribed on gift tags and tied to the leg of every old hope.

I detailed for Jeremy my first home built on the back of the 1940 truck. Then I went on to describe our second dwelling in a Berkeley apartment house. The rent was fifteen dollars a month.

"It was one of two closets or storage rooms in the basement. Its dimensions were only large enough to hold a mattress and an unconnected stove." I remembered the children who had asked me to move out so they could rent it for a clubhouse.

"I had one chair which I used to pull up to the Tappan range door, which when open was my desk. Those were the days when I wrote my first full journals. . . ."

Anna interrupted, thrusting her head between us from the back seat.

"Matthew brought his rubber raft. You told him not to, but he's got it hidden under the seat."

Matthew's response was much like a pretzel. He twisted around talking salty.

"You didn't say I couldn't bring it, but said you didn't recommend it. There's a lot of difference."

His sister was reduced to one guttural "Huh," which Matthew repeated.

Before I could wonder at Jeremy's response, he turned and rebuked them in a quiet voice that was full of thunder. I was relieved to see that with children he could be an iron fist in a velvet glove.

The interruptions drained my enthusiasm for continuing. I decided not to bother to tell Jeremy during this ride about the refurbished chicken coop, or the basement, or garage, that had all been my residence at one time.

Once the highway bordered the Pacific Ocean, clouds began to gather while the wind labored to push any loose ones into a single mass. At the beach, I had everyone take their jacket. The children ran down to the shore hoping to spot a seal on a rock. They caused several birds to take flight to a safe distance, where they resumed their occupation of moving back and forth as if on tiny wheels with the direction of the waves.

Jeremy and I took a blanket and spread it out on a niche within the dunes.

I asked him if his two unmarried children would ever live with us.

"Only for very brief visits," was his firm reply.

He explained that Gloria had just moved back to Minnesota after living with him in Southern California.

"She has always worked in my office, but I wanted her to try college. And Patty wants Jessie, our youngest daughter, to stay close to her."

Jeremy's voice trailed off as if the subject had some additional small print that was only his to read.

I turned my head from looking at him up to the gray gauze of the sky, pondering our dialogues. A lot of what we said resembled a kind of verbal card game. The past was our own hand which we would define for the other. And the deck was our future waiting between us to be drawn.

"Jeremy," I said. "I've been thinking that everyone has a moment in life to be famous. Maybe it's having one's name drawn from a revolving drum and announced over a microphone in a shopping center contest."

I ran my fingers through the sand while trying to think of examples.

"Or walking into a friend's house to find a surprise party organized in your honor—but whatever it is, the experience seems to come in some form."

"Yeah," Jeremy replied. I suspected only his outer ear was listening.

"When one publishes a book, an author is famous for about fifteen minutes. I'm almost done and by the time I move to Los Angeles my quarter hour will have passed of going to speak to groups and answer questions in microphones. I'll be able to live quietly again in a normal life."

"I doubt that," he said while reaching over and touching my brow. As he traced the contour of my cheekbone below my eye, Anna loomed at our side. She seemed to fill the horizon.

"There you are! I've been looking for you. I have to go to the bathroom."

She must have read some of my reluctance for she became more explicit with her need.

"Number two, really bad!"

Jeremy said that he thought he remembered a gas station a few miles back. I took my daughter's hand and ran with her to the car.

Once I returned, I found Mary Elisabeth wrapped up in my side of the blanket next to Jeremy. She said she was cold so I sent her back to the beach to find her coat. Before she was out of sight, an isolated drop of rain fell, making a perfect circle in the sand. It had a small ridge on one side formed by its impact. Another landed inches away, making it necessary for us to cover ourselves. Propped up on elbows, we watched the dunes darken with rain. The wind, having once succeeded in knocking the clouds together, now seemed to direct its attention to the citizens of the beach and blew with the same fury it had used in the upper regions of the sky. The rain, synchronized with the attack, began to pelt us. We ran for the children and the car.

Neither Matthew nor the girls had given any thought to staying dry. It must be the law of attraction between children and bodies of water. I found their shoes cast up on the beach without any pattern but abandon. They were playing the ancient game of chasing the old wave back into the ocean and daring the new one to catch them. Their saturated cuffs showed a high tally of points in favor of the sea.

When I told them we had to go, they began to grumble at the idea of leaving so soon. Once their minds left the rhythm of the waters to thinking about their own wet state, their complaint changed to how uncomfortable they felt. I thought how their cry at birth had not been one of praise for leaving the womb's dark waters. It was a complaint from the start that has only learned to better articulate its grievances. I could feel my own attitude wanting back the crevice in the dunes.

Jeremy asked to drive. He slid behind the steering wheel and requested the ignition key. I checked all of my pockets, my purse, and the dashboard with no sign of the brown leather tab attached to my Toyota key. I felt a furthering of my irritation. I would nominate for the

Nobel Prize any doctor who could attach brain cells to a right hand that would do nothing but remember where one put things. Matthew asked Jeremy if he knew how to hot-wire the starter. To him it would be worth it to have lost the key entirely if he could watch that basic principle of mechanics. Instead Jeremy suggested we reconstruct my movements. When I had returned with Anna from the bathroom, he recalled that I ran up the hill.

Jeremy went out into the rain to trace my path back to the dunes. Marveling at his cheerfulness, I felt a fresh confidence that I was marrying the right man. Anna suggested that this might be an opportunity to live on the beach, build a shelter with driftwood and catch fish for our sustenance. Jeremy returned with the familiar key ring in his hand.

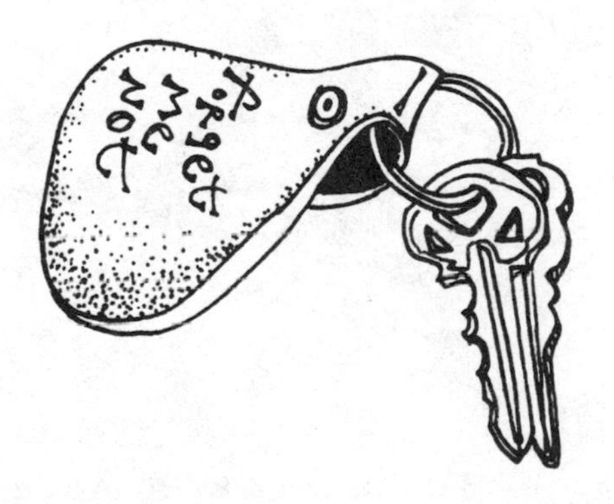

As we pulled onto the highway I read the mileage sign to the city and sighed. I really didn't want to go home. I decided to try and explain the feeling to Jeremy of not belonging anymore to Portland, but yet not grafted to the new life of being a wife.

"If these days were a double feature, we are sitting through the credits of the old movie and just waiting for the second to be wound upon the reel."

I looked out at the hills dark with fir trees at our horizon. They looked like scallops torn by hand and pasted along a line. I organized a plan. After dropping Jeremy at the airport I would get sleeping bags and the necessary clothes to take the children camping until the beginning of school.

Since the wedding was to be a new chapter, I wanted to seize the time it takes for the old page to revolve through the air and spend what I could of it in the country.

August 24

"What will it be like when we're married, Mother?"

Anna was waiting for me on the bank of a stream. She had piled several flat rocks in front of her tennis shoes. In an underarm swing she shot one into the water. Hoping to skip it, she turned to me when her missile didn't reappear for a second arc above the water.

Pulling off my knapsack, I sat beside her. I recognized the plural form she used in phrasing her question with the word "we."

"We can't really know. It will be real life with adjustments and adaptations, though."

I didn't want the children to think that the structure of our days in Los Angeles was going to be formed by multiplying sugar crystals. Having a husband and a father wasn't going to be a living manifestation of such sweetness that we would each need our own box of refrigerated insulin. I tried to explain that tangible goals or hopes should be held lightly and not seen as ultimate solutions to what we are.

I knew I had lost her. Anna's eyes fell to the stones that she had gathered. She began to arrange them in a circle.

I tried again. One block of truth should be tall enough for scholars and yet have proportions that children can understand.

"Remember, Anna, when you wanted to go to camp more than anything in the world? You taped the brochure on the wall by the bed. You chanted, 'Daily swimming, campfires every night,' as if each event was a separate color of the rainbow.

"But the camp itself was a different experience from what you had expected. There was poison oak and a quarreling roommate.

"Adults are like that, too. Some spend their whole lives deeply wishing to own more than what they have."

I reached out to touch her.

"But they are mistaken.
Circumstances are no permanent cure
to what we are inside."

I pulled some pink blooms off a stalk of foxgloves. Through years in the forest it had reached a height where it flowered above my waist. I had taken the children to a retreat camp at Silver Creek Falls. The facility included one-room cabins and a central lodge. Anna reached over to take the flowers from me and put them on her fingertips. Since the blossoms looked like bonnets, she flexed her hand, creating five fingers bowing.

Without looking up at me, Anna had one last question.

"Will Jeremy Foster leave us if he doesn't like us?"

I knew her query was like a two-headed eagle that stares in opposite directions at once. Her father's abrupt and permanent departure was one side of her experience, and based on that, she was looking into the future.

Anna needed reassurance.

"You will hear us pledge to stay with each other."

I explained that both Jeremy and I would promise in front of God and everyone who comes, not to leave the other no matter what happens. I chanted sickness, health, richer, poorer, better, worse.

The child visibly brightened.

"That's it!" she said. She began to think of all her friends who lived in a one-parent family due to divorce.

"Everyone who gets married should make that kind of promise." Anna felt she had uncovered the answer to one of the ills of the world.

September 10

I pulled out Jeremy's wedding invitation list from an oversize manila envelope. I was somewhat uncomfortable with its order. There was not a smudge on the paper. The two columns were double-spaced for easy reading without any evidence of second thoughts that would be indicated by a crossed-out name, or two added at the bottom with a ball-point. The package had arrived at my porch much earlier than any late burst of frantic motivation that was familiar to my own style.

By contrast, I had an address book of sepia papers laced by some craftsman between two sheets of myrtlewood. I treated it like a box, having thrown between its covers any paper scrap that was ever used for recording names with numbers. I had used corners of maps and edges of paper napkins. It was full of the left-hand corners torn off envelopes.

I went down to the stationery store to inquire about having invitations printed. I refused the salesman's first suggestion to be modern. Most couples now, he explained, have a photograph of themselves together embossed onto the page. Internally, I reviewed a rapid succession of possible shots that were the milestones of our courtship. We stood smiling at the ocean dripping with rain, or earlier, covered with volcano dust.

In turn, the clerk gave me several enormous sample books filled with alternate styles. To each page were cemented two envelopes, one fitting within the other. I wondered if the tradition wasn't a midnight thought of some manufacturer looking toward increasing his profits and reducing his surplus stock. If the effect was to be for suspense, tissue papers to be fitted over the type were also included.

With my choice, I submitted to the salesman a small

hand-drawn map to the Silver Creek retreat center for reproduction. I indicated with my pen the gravel road that leads to the chapel on the property.

Considering part of my shopping to be the stamp itself, I went to the small neighborhood post office created in the back of a drugstore. To my request for special-issue designs, I was passed a sheet vivid with squares of orange color. In the center was a message commemorating an educational philosophy. In capital letters it read, "Learning Never Ends." I bought a small number for those I felt had the eye to receive it on a wedding invitation.

After putting my purchases in the front seat, I slid behind the steering wheel. I thought how the wedding date had once been a dot in the distant landscape of autumn. Now it had form and was beginning to race into view. My image made the wedding seem like a locomotive set in motion by our promise.

I took the keys from my purse and put them in the ignition. I wondered about our lives once we were transported to the south. There would be the problem of forming a new family identity. Somehow I thought of it evolving through dinner table conversations pushed up to breakfast settings and linked to the folded napkins of yet another meal together. I caught my eye's reflection while adjusting the rearview mirror. The look was one of anticipation of the vision of a new life.

September 20

Dropping the bath towel over the sink, I studied my reflection in the mirror. My abdomen was crossed by two prominent and lengthy scars. My body was a living hospital chart. The longest incision was for removing my spleen. The second scar was at a sixty-degree angle across my hip into the pit of my abdomen. Looking down, I carried a giant letter "V." I wondered, when married, how my husband would read it. It could either stand for "Victim," recipient of modern plague, or "Victory—" I'm alive.

The borders of all my radiation fields were marked by tattoos. They ran up and down my body like large grains of black pepper permanently caught under my skin. I counted the spots in the mirror: two on my neck, six on my breasts, and six on my abdomen.

It was only the pending marriage that made me care. For the first time it mattered to me that I deviated from a normal creation. I encouraged my reflection in a theory; bodies are nothing but automobiles and the real passenger is inside. To further my comfort, I spoke to myself.

"So what if you've got some fender damage and rust spots."

Our house has one bathroom. Matthew was outside the door, bare-chested in his pajama bottoms. "I could hear you talking to yourself," he said.

He walked by me and closed the door with a last remark: "I bet Jeremy Foster is going to end up thinking that you are completely crazy."

Turning into my room, I wondered why, at certain times, circumstances are exactly like a chair. Both humor and a kind of sorrow race to take the seat. I didn't know whether to laugh or to cry, and both seemed appropriate.

September 23

The medical school has a population of doctors that are like shifting desert sand. There would be a new formation in my afternoon visit as the residents rotated through several departments in a year. I thought of the examination rooms as part of the wasteland, a place where cancer patients wander, feeling at a distance from anything familiar.

I unfolded my appointment slip for the hematology clinic and gave it to the volunteer. Only three months had elapsed since my last physical examination, but I had to fulfill the examination requirements for an Oregon marriage license. Choosing the end seat on a couch, I regarded the people already waiting to be called in to a physician. Most of them were scheduled for dosages of chemotherapy. The magazine pages had been turned such a maximum of times that the paper resembled bills of money that had been long in circulation.

Hearing the words, "wheat grass" and "apricot pits," I looked up at the two men sitting across from me. They were discussing alternate diet therapies in contrast to the toxics of chemotherapy. Those kinds of paragraphs, including talk of laetrile, were the thoughts that lived under the cushions in all the waiting rooms I've known for hospital cancer treatments. Some stagger toward them as a tributary of hope coupled with the need to do something for oneself in order to feel a measure of control.

The sound of the nurse's cart being pushed on the other side of the back wall made me shudder. I thought of its rattles as the bottles themselves crying out because the toxic chemicals were splashing against their sides in transit between rooms. It was only twenty-one months since the last tourniquet had been fitted to my arm and the professional fingers squeezed my flesh looking for an adequate vein.

Not knowing I would recover from my relapse, I had tried to see my months of dying as a peculiar privilege. If death is a station in space and the common destination, it's preferable to have some time to pack for it. I would want to leave the children a lot of last-minute instructions.

Instead, I wondered at the mystery of how I was sitting with a state medical form in my purse requiring a doctor's signature so I could be a bride. Maybe future events sit around the corner from my predictions laughing at me because I forgot again that nothing is impossible.

It was such a prolonged time of waiting that when my name was called, I had to stir myself to remember why I had come.

Grover Bagby came through the door, accompanied by a second-year resident. Dr. Bagby was a staff member who had been one of my overseeing physicians through both sieges of illness. He took a seat on a small stool set on wheels which he pulled over to the examination table. After telling him I was getting married, he wanted to review one detail.

"At the time your spleen was removed, your ovaries were pulled over to midline where they could be shielded from abdominal radiation. This means that there is a slight chance that you can get pregnant."

"No," I protested, suppressing a laugh. I explained that all my menstrual cycles had ceased after the laparotomy operation.

Doctors can't be wrong. Like weathermen and politicians, they can pad themselves with percentages.

"That doesn't mean that all ovarian function stopped," added Dr. Bagby.

The resident asked me to raise my arms so he could palpate for any swollen lymph nodes. His style was to try and tickle one to the surface. I think it was the only time that I ever left the hematology clinic laughing.

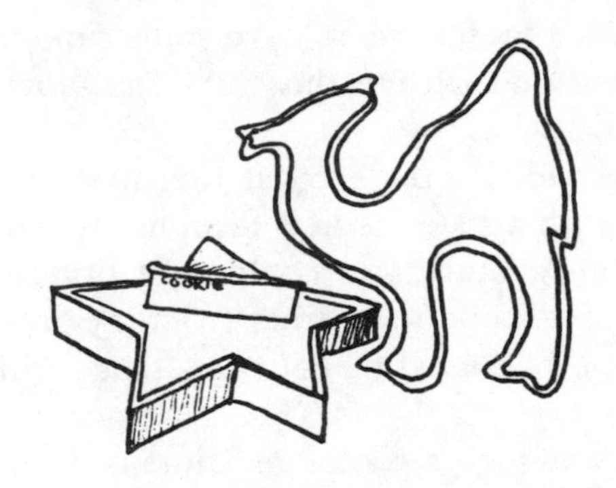

October 1

It had become my habit to bring cardboard boxes home from the grocery store. Thrown into the basement, they grew in number and bulk. The contents of the house had to be completely packed by the wedding date for shipping to Los Angeles. I chanted, "Less than a month," whenever I needed a stimulant.

While I put kitchen utensils into a box I thought, moving is the revelation of excess. I counted three can openers with different colored handles. I had a drawer full of cookie cutters as numerous as common nouns. Fishing out the bottom three, I added a turkey, tree, and heart to my carton. I found trays for freezing water into any size of cube. There was a hand press for garlic and another for fresh parsley. Since we only need to eat, sleep, and clothe ourselves, the infinity of my props for survival seemed staggering. Peering at the number of coats in my front hall closet I decided that the Bedouin nomad is much closer to the right idea. I'm only changing camps and it seems more in line to load a single camel than trucks designed with suspension for holding several tons. With utmost pleasure, I envisioned giving away a lot that I owned.

I decided that it would be my good-bye salute to Portland's thrift stores. Having frequented certain low-cost bins and racks, I would make a temporary outlet on Couch Street.

Opening the first of the sacks that would be free to any visitor, I put in two can openers and kept one. I thought of a certain single mother that might want the turkey cookie cutter.

Hoping Melanie was still at home, I dialed her kitchen, then pulled out the measuring-cup drawer to sort with one hand. I threw four green cups into a bag that were once the free spring gift from Lincoln Savings.

"Let me come and help you," Melanie said.

"Now that I'm moving I won't need any of the necessities noted in 'Better Living Catalog.' "

I quoted from memory, " 'Digital diet loafers provide by an attachment to each shoe a constant read-out of body weight with every step.' "

"Laurel, I'm going to call around and see if others can come over too."

"Listen," I said. " 'These can be programmed to give an audible warning when undesired weight variations occur, thus providing an embarrassment factor incentive to keep one's weight at a certain level.' "

"I'll try Arlene and I know Margo's home. . . ."

October 18

Standing at the curb, I looked up at my house. The porch light had just switched on. The hall light was next. Its glow instantly illuminated the rectangles of glass set to the sides of the front door. It was my mother who had arrived three days earlier. I could watch her progress from the porch through to the upstairs. She had taken over the small jobs that kept a house functioning so that I could finish evacuating all the loose contents into boxes.

Putting the key into the car's ignition, I resented the tyranny of small details that had stormed my mind with banners reading "Urgent." So numerous were their ranks that they had tried to grab the chairs from the more noble, but slower, thoughts. But at last, Jeremy is coming, I thought.

The airport is set among the fields by the Columbia River. The highway goes by an acre planted with pumpkins. In the streetlight I could see the sign's large silhouette of a wooden farmer pushing a wheelbarrow. Someone had stenciled the name "Jim" across his overalls. There were no stars, but the moon illuminated in its disk the rapid flight of moving clouds. After parking the car, I sucked the night air deep into my lungs. I thought how the stability that marked Jeremy would soon be spread over all of our lives like a garment.

Once inside the double doors of the terminal entrance, I could hear the public address system. It was a woman's voice telling flight details in the tone that lacked all animation. It reminded me of the same lifeless enunciation that gives recorded telephone information. On the escalator up to the ticket floor the monotone continued naming carriers, giving flight numbers, and announcing that the airplanes were leaving early from a given gate. After the third broadcast of a premature departure, I went

to the Northwest Airlines booth to ask for an explanation.

"It's the volcano," was the attendant's reply. Another plume of ash had been discharged into the atmosphere, and based on the first reports of wind direction, Portland was in its path.

I remembered how the airport had been closed before, and public metropolitan life had all but ceased in the rain of fallout. I laid that image across the wedding. It provoked a first concern for the out-of-state guests who would be flying in for the ceremony. Every detail was threatened if the result of the eruption was going to be another massive outpouring of ash.

Seriously mulling these things, I went to the gate to meet Jeremy. I could graph my concern for the weather as his plane taxied into a position to be connected with the accordion door. It had been my headline thought. Searching through the first passengers for Jeremy's face, it decreased to a front-page story. The new large-cap headline read, "FOSTER ARRIVES." When I spotted him and began to wave, all of the volcano bulletins shrank to one paragraph on the back page of my news.

I thought about us as we walked to the luggage with our arms interlocked. If we had been asked to give our age without any personal knowledge of a chronological number and with no available data but feelings, I would have said we were beginning our twenties.

October 19

One state of being asleep is much like being under a kind of dark water. Dreams are strangely lit caverns under this sea, glimpsed and forgotten in all the currents of a night's rest. By morning, I'm barely under the surface, with my shoulder or an elbow coming out of the water while I turn in my bed. I sat up quoting a nursery rhyme:

> Pockets full of poseys,
> Ashes, ashes, we all fall down.

I turned with a start to the window. It was a late autumn morning. The leaves were crumpled with color. Most had left the trees and lay in drifts across the backyard. There was no evidence of any volcano dust. The wind must have changed direction in the night.

My mother was already up. I've always known her to be the first out of bed seasoning a house with coffee and maybe a cigarette. It was almost as if I could see her through the floor, filling the holes in the children's clothes with thread and clucking at my use of safety pins.

In the afternoon, I met with Jeremy to get an authorized marriage license. Receiving legal accreditation is much like the old game of "scavenger hunt."

Because of the weekend, it was the last hour that we could get our forms for Monday's ceremony. True to the rules of the game, we had been given a list of things that had to be brought to the county desk in order to get our prize paper. Jeremy handed all of the completed forms to the Multnomah County Clerk. Her office cubicle was next to the window where one enrolled a pet for a city dog tag.

After turning over the medical sheets, and checking for the doctor's signature, she asked to see our witness. She explained that a third person was necessary to substantiate that all our data were factual.

We stared back at her. The office would be closed if we took the time to drive back to my neighborhood and fasten a friend into the back seat.

"Oh, we'll be right back," said Jeremy.

Without a word, the clerk wrinkled her lip, which operated with the rhythm of a wave upon her face. It set in motion her nose which adjusted her glasses. She must have developed the mannerism through years of having her hands filled with papers.

We took the elevator down to the street and walked out on the pavement looking for any friendly, slow-moving pedestrian. Everyone had a brisk pace with eyes set ahead to appointments and solitary destinies.

Across the street was a large religious bookstore. It was the symbol on the sign that compelled me to suggest it. In capital letters, it read, "Crossroads," with a two-line drawing of one path being intersected by another.

All shop clerks initiate their professional services with the tune, "May I help you?" It's the ancient song of buying and selling.

I explained to the manager that we didn't need a thing, but only to borrow a person for eight charitable minutes. Neither his eyes nor his mouth changed. It was the eyebrows that registered the request. They rose slightly into his forehead, as if not sure that that could be allowed.

The walls surrounding our conversation were filled with books. In a showcase below him were a number of Bible translations opened for comparative study to the Sermon on the Mount.

I hoped the line "Give to him who asks of thee," which was blocked in red, would rise from the text in an invisible cloud. I wanted the vapor to enshroud his bald head and seep into his memory.

"Our stockman, Bill, is on a coffee break. Maybe he will go across the street with you."

In the Multnomah County elevator, Bill began to reminisce about his own wedding. He said, "The ordained minister kept cracking his knuckles as we pledged our union." I knew Bill's sentence had divided between us. It split in two parts. Jeremy was thinking about the clergyman cracking his knuckles, while I was wondering about some woman standing at attention with her hand over her heart:

I pledge allegiance
To this man named Bill
And to this house
In which I'll stand,
One vacuum cleaner,
Dust invisible,
With regular meals
And clean sheets
For all.

The clerk sniffed at our bogus witness. He signed his name according to her instruction and disappeared out the glass door.

The marriage license had a small drawing of a wagon train on the Oregon Trail. I saw it as our ticket of passage to a new frontier.

October 20

Still in my nightgown, I went and slipped in bed with Mary Elisabeth. I had first heard her voice coming out from her room, bouncing along the wall about the same level as the children's fingerprints. She was wearing her favorite sleeper, but a growth spurt had recently required me to snip off the cloth feet that were a part of the total garment.

"Well," I said, "I'm getting married tonight."

"I want to get married, too," was her reply.

The object of her interest was another four-year-old named Jason Scheidler. Her idea of wedded life was to be set free from the obligation of afternoon naps. Reluctant to get up from her side, I wanted to hold that last flavor of us waking together in Portland.

I don't know what other women do on the morning of their wedding day. Maybe they luxuriate in some detail of personal grooming. Perhaps they choose a beauty shop so their hair can be heated and bent into curls. From years of newsprint dailies, I saw all the one-inch faces of newspaper brides having the time for a slow bath in waters swirled with Avon oils.

As for me, I had to drive for some last errands, and go into the basement to finish taping the boxes for the moving van that was scheduled to come in three days.

As I pulled out into the traffic on Glisan, the sun

emerged from the clouds flooding the street with light and shadows. I had been bidding Portland good-bye for weeks, recording visual images on some internal rack of postcards. Looking up at the mountains, I took one last shot of mist and vapors. I knew I would need to carry the memory of moisture into Los Angeles.

My father took the car keys from me at the curb. I could read "irritation" in the creases of his face. It was a characteristic tightening and deepening of lines etching into his eyes and mouth. My parents were taking the three children to a motel near Silverton. The details of barrettes and small white socks were beginning to take their toll. I stood with him until everyone got in the car with their clothes wrapped in filmy dry cleaner plastics. I watched them drive away, reminding myself that I wouldn't be at that wheel again until some undetermined date when I retrieved my vehicle from their Fremont garage.

Jeremy had already arrived and was taping up the last boxes. I found him balancing on one knee, his forehead shiny from labor. Every man sweats differently; perspiration is as diverse as fingerprints. Jeremy's brow looked as if it had been recently wiped with vegetable oil.

"Mexican beaches," I said, directly addressing his exertions. It was a spoonful of thought from the bottle of excitement within me.

Jeremy wanted to know the hour we were expected for the afternoon rehearsal.

I left the house for the last time much as I had always left it, rushing to an appointment. Inside me was a profound respect for the fact that I was crossing to the other side.

I met Arlene in the gravel parking lot by the chapel. She had been watching for me with a message. We had pulled in the stall next to my car so I knew my parents would be waiting in the sanctuary with other members of the wedding.

She looked me in the eye. "Don't get upset . . ."

When anyone begins a sentence cautioning me to avoid angers and depression, they cut the elevator cord on my spirit and I begin to sink immediately.

"It's Matthew," she said. "He forgot all of his good clothes, and only has what he is wearing."

It didn't matter to me. I didn't want one detail to become like a balloon and be blown up beyond proportions.

Once in the church, I sought out my son. In the morning he had based his choice of wardrobe on the principle of opposites: By night he knew he would be forced into a starched shirt and tie; therefore, what portion of the day would belong to him, he was going to be comfortable. In a T-shirt, he stood between his sisters in their red velvet dresses. The shirt had one small hole at the seam by the sleeve and below it was the line "No Trespassing."

With the exception of my parents and the girls, we were all still in Levis.

I was to take my things to a cabin up the hill from the chapel to dress. My suit, sealed into a plastic sack like an enormous white bread sandwich, was hanging on a hook above the car window. I looked for the bag with my matching shoes and underwear. It wasn't on the seat or floor. The trunk was empty except for the spare tire and jacket. Somehow it must have been forgotten in our haste. Walking with Arlene to the cabin, I had the idea that my missing things had left with Matthew's suit just "as the dish ran away with the spoon. . . ."

"You must be nervous," replied Arlene after listening to me quote the Mother Goose line. She told me to take my shower while she tried to locate some kind of acceptable replacement.

I had to laugh at the alternatives waiting for me on the couch. It was the underpants that were the most startling by contrast. Instead of my silk and lace purchase, there was now a pair of ribbed combed cotton that had legs extending to above the knee. Their weight was an extrathick gauge of cotton, whereas mine were so light that they could have floated off the department store counter. The top of my wedding blouse was lace set with satin-covered buttons. Not having my special-purchase brassiere, I had to cut down the cups with a scissors so the bra wouldn't show, which left a ragged, fraying edge. My reflection looked like some backwoods bride who couldn't get all of her mail-order clothes. All that I needed was licorice gum to conceal a front and canine tooth.

In a closet, Arlene had found anonymous white pumps which were enormous on my feet. The straps arched above my foot, even after punching the buckle through the last hole. My foot sloshed on the shiny plastic sole. I refused to wear them and put back on my black suede heels that I had been wearing all afternoon.

My hair was still wet fifteen minutes before I was due at the chapel. I decided to blame the mass popularity of the "I Love Lucy" television show that had dominated the network ratings during the fifties. It was my early imprinting of situation comedy that had damaged me.

Messengers came to whisper about the crowd that had gathered in excess of any seating. There was going to be a throng standing at the back. Arlene left to accompany on the piano two of her oldest children who were to play their violins.

I stood at the mirror braiding portions of my hair, inserting into my plaits wild flowers that I had picked last August and dried by hanging them from a hook in my basement.

I chose the longest path that winds through a hillside of ferns, tied like dark knots in the evening's shadows. The ground was cushioned from the very age of the forest; first a lake, then a meadow, and eons of years later, a woods. My feelings were detached from any urgency. I had no sense of haste. Even my excitement was replaced by a state of calm. It was as if the importance of the hour was stretching me to a plane that exists without time.

"I am a bride," I thought, and wanted to fold the idea across the prophecy for the end of the world when the Savior comes as the groom.

My trail merged with the larger pathway connecting the parking lot down to the chapel. I could see its cedar sides and the flower beds bathed in light from the open doors.

My father was among the people at the back. I took his arm to walk slowly, holding my eyes to the front, wanting to break rank and hug friends I could see in the sweep of peripheral vision.

Jeremy's face stood out, full of safety, and my eyes anchored on him. We stood together.

Pastor Hanson wanted to make room for the numbers at the back. He invited all the children to the front. We were married in the midst of little people sitting on the stairs, touching their shoes, playing with their pockets. I saw that someone had found Matthew a brown cowboy dress shirt with pearl snap buttons.

Once we walked out as the Fosters triumphant, Mary Elisabeth followed us. Marching behind us in the aisle,

she waited until we stood yards from the church and were engulfed in the shadows from the woods. She brushed Jeremy's leg for attention:

"Are you my Daddy now?"

"Well, yes," he said, surprised as I was to see her.

She ran at his legs with both hands extended, then pulled back shouting, "Catch me then!" and ran toward the church where my mother apprehended her.

I saw a number of single mothers, including Melanie, sitting together at one of the reception's round wood tables. Their plates were dappled with second helpings from the spread of meats and salads. One speared a shrimp and said, laughing, "You're not one of us anymore."

Oh, I am, I thought. I am everything I have ever been. It's as if several lives make one. I am the wild daughter, cancer victim, mother alone. *There is a time and season for every kind of understanding.*

People greeted us, the wandering host and hostess to all our company. Unwittingly picking up an imitation of a predominant accent, I wanted to congratulate the guests.

Jeremy's son and two blond daughters sat in a row

to eat. His youngest girl, Jessie, had stayed in Minnesota. Having just met them a few days before the ceremony, I yearned to sit with them. Watching them talk among themselves, I recognized that the history of literature has been unfair in its traditional definition of "stepmothers."

There's a lot of bad press, I thought, for stepmothers and alligators.

As we drove to our Portland hotel, I kept repeating in the confines of my mind, "I'm a married woman . . ."

October 21

I woke up feeling my husband's legs entwined between my own like a vine. I didn't want to move, taking care not to disturb him.

It was my thirty-fifth birthday, and I was given to recollections. Once I was old enough to recognize the cycle of a birthdate, it became a personal visit to that tree within myself that gets a new ring once a year. I've seen monuments in the California Redwoods, great slices of trunk tilted for a display. Dates and events are recorded on small tags within the lines of its circumference: Marco Polo, Columbus discovers America. I had my own history. Last year I was speaking at 9:00 and 11:00 at a rural church. Between those hours, all the adults and children were gathered into the Sunday school auditorium. There, the superintendent asked, "Who has a birthday?"

My hand flew up before I thought. Then I was compelled to come forward with two little children. We were asked to drop the number of our new age in pennies into a bank while everyone sang to us. The bank was a white plastic church with a slit behind the steeple. The five- and seven-year-old were done quickly and could resume their seats. I didn't have thirty-four coins and had to be bailed out by the lady playing the piano.

Jeremy turned over, binding me to his side with his arm. I wondered if we were both awake and feigning a stillness for the sake of the other. I could study his hand. It was the first time I had seen it without any flicker of movement. His fingertips rested on the gold hotel sheet. Uniform creases from a professional ironing service made a rectangle around his imprint.

The day I turned thirty-three was during a week's cycle of pills for chemotherapy. With some other women, I had driven to a cabin with hiking knapsacks. The owner dropped by to ask if I wouldn't take an hour to visit her neighbor who was dying of cancer.

The year before that I took the children ice skating at an indoor rink.

Age thirty-one was celebrated in New York. My publishing friends took me to the Four Seasons Restaurant. The logo on the menu and matchbook showed a stylized tree with just a few leaves left.

The celebration of age thirty was done on a circular track with stations only at my couch and bed.

Jeremy's breathing changed from silence to a continuing sound that matched in its rhythmic measures. It was his exhalation that had a certain marked propulsion. I could see his briefcase against the couch which held our midmorning flight tickets to Mexico. In a salute to our plans, on impulse, I tapped my gold band on his. It was a toast to the future, and the sound and movement woke him.

Puerto Vallerta, Mexico, October 24

To me, there's something about water that has some of the same properties as the mystery of sleep. A night's rest is the passage between exhaustion and stamina. Likewise, all bathing has a quality of renewal. It seemed appropriate that we were either in bed or in the sea for the genesis of our marriage.

I ran back to the hotel room to get some fruit to eat with Jeremy on the beach. I paused by the doorframe and surveyed our room. One small, harmless lizard clung to the wall where it made a right angle with the adjacent wall.

Our toiletries at the sink, garments, and shoes were left like two distinct fingerprints. His swirls didn't match mine in the care of our possessions. I have what I call "middle-clothes" which, worn once, are not dirty, and are about to be used again. I put them on the backs of chairs and bathroom hooks. All of my husband's habiliments hung from hangers in an even row. His shirts were all together, followed by another unit of trousers. I thought it could be worse; he could believe in color-coding them on the rack, with a three-finger separation between hangers.

At the sink was Jeremy's brown leather box with a zipper lid. He used it as a miniature medicine cabinet. We still had two tubes of toothpaste; his was returned after use, while mine lay on the tiles as a work of sculpture. It had distinct twists and folds created by my pressure points. I always lose the cap, leaving a definite hole, opening into space. Once unscrewed, the cap disappears to wander forever through the waste places with the lost bobby pins and an occasional pierced earring. For transport, I have to put the Crest tube into a plastic sandwich sack.

I took the time to gather up my left sandal from the couch and the other one by the bed to stow in the closet. As I picked up a jacket from a chair to put away, I thought that the sharing of our lives could not help but reveal some rough edges. If I am a board, then I suspect that I bear certain stains, like the oval discolorations of watermarks left on me from carrying certain pressures. There's no doubt that the marks of my experiences from long times of stress need refinishing. I wryly thought that the traditional tool of such an enterprise is sandpaper.

Taking some mangoes and bananas from the dresser, I felt our adaptations consigned to the future. Our love seemed to have just a language of peace without corrections. Some, I knew, were disappointed in honeymoons, but I wasn't. I had waited a long time for intimacy.

Mexico City, October 28

Seeing the crowds around the shopwindows, I asked Jeremy to cross the street with me. I wanted to know what held the attention of so many people, prompting the ones in the back to alternately stand on their toes, then bend down to look for a passage through the press of hipbones.

As we stepped off the curb, I recalled a similar crowd once watching a television set in a village store window. The black-and-white screen showed a horse stepping up and down in place to the music of a Mexican hat dance. We, as a couple, were young enough in our relationship to still be sharing portions of our personal history, and old enough to have vast amounts not yet revealed.

We joined the outer circle under the store sign that translated, "Bakery." As others came to stand behind us, we were caught and pinned up to the hot backs of the pedestrians. Some of the men had perspiration marks staining their shirts, making damp blobs on the cotton like personal maps of tropical continents. I recognized the fact that I didn't feel well. The state of being in remission makes me pinpoint and probe any malfunction for its cause. I blamed my low-level nausea on unfamiliar spices.

In the window was a single wooden coffin. A woman whose pallor was enhanced by stage makeup was laid to rest in a white funeral gown. Flanked by candles, her breaths were too shallow to be detected. In the adjoining display window were ceramic figures duplicating a graveside burial in the scale size of model railroad props. What held the audience were the sporadic movements of the woman in the coffin. Without opening her eyes, she threw out candy at the people inside the shop. Through the glass I could see them scream, and then dart for the cellophane-wrapped sweets. Occasionally a tray of buns was knocked to the floor, and store personnel returned it to the display table.

Even after we went inside, my nausea kept drawing my perceptions away from the skull-and-crossbone cookies to my own weakness. Waves of illness kept washing through me. From weeks of chemotherapy I had made subjective categories of nausea. While pain is a distinct bite, nausea is more liquid in its discomfort, immersing the whole self. I wanted to go outside and find a place to sit.

I went to look for Jeremy. A mechanical witch was riding a track suspended from the ceiling, above the customers in the aisles. I found my husband taking photographs of enormous Halloween cakes. All aspects of death were reproduced in the stiffly iced confections. It looked like a progression for lost souls carved in sugar. Beside graveyards and tombstones was a red cavern with plastic devils stuck into the folds of the crimson topping.

Because of the intensity of my physical discomfort, I wanted to go anywhere to lie down. It seemed a necessity to close my eyes and avoid all external stimuli. Jeremy led me to the large central park where I collapsed on the first stretch of lawn. As I adjusted my body to irregularities in the grass, my husband leaned over me to whisper, "I want you to know that if you die, it's going to ruin my whole afternoon."

After a rest I felt better. It was like the returning tide that lifts up the ship from the shallows. Still there was a certain queasiness, and I dreaded elevators and taxis that accelerate on corners.

October 30

After checking our luggage we sat in the departure lounge for the flight to Los Angeles. I watched a tour group from Japan pat their souvenirs. Most had purchased exaggerated felt sombreros embroidered with gold spangles. One brushed his thumb over the end of elongated bull horns mounted on a board.

My husband had gravitated to his briefcase. It was a time to reorder his mind for going to the office in the afternoon. Jeremy was engrossed in some papers. He had taken out his reading glasses and abstractedly clicked their ear extensions together before putting them on.

Moods are the weather of the soul. Although I wanted to see our house, I felt anxious about the transition. It was almost a tiny knot of distress about reemerging into regular life. I didn't want to watch my husband pack off in the morning to the commuter freeway, and for me to start tracking through strange Southern California supermarkets.

The flight was announced in Spanish, then, without pause, in rapid English. Taking a seat by the window, I noticed how the light accentuated innumerable scratches on its exterior. I thought that the three windowpanes in my view looked like miniature ice-skating ponds standing on end. The abrasions were short, silver intersecting lines.

I didn't like leaving Mexico. My emotion, which ignores all reason, wanted us to continue living together on foreign soil as if we were posing for the Harlequin series of romance novels. Since the back covers always quote a line from the contents, I felt Jeremy's statement that "few ever know such a love as this" had more impact on a beach than while I was reaching into an open refrigerator.

In the galley was a final monitoring of aluminum-wrapped food trays by an airline caterer. The stewardess was taking her last private minutes before she would have to start again and demonstrate the use of oxygen masks and seat belts.

I wanted my husband to make a gesture that he understood, or to give me some look of reluctance at ending our first days where there were no diversions but the other. Instead, he moved over to the aisle in order to utilize the middle seat as an additional filing cabinet for his works in progress.

I took a magazine in an effort to shake myself free from the weed of excessive romanticism. It's a fast-growing plant that can strangle the garden of relationships.

From the beverage cart I accepted juice and a roll in respect to a theorem on mental health: we are potentially more disturbed when tired or hungry.

Immediately a deep abdominal pain which had been in embers reignited. In response to the internal burning, I squeezed my napkin and armrest in a kind of grip that used my nails as acupuncture. It was the Portland doctor's office that I pictured. I could visualize walking into the medical school clinic and getting a prescription. The right medication is viewed by someone in pain as water for thirst. I found that all of Peter Pan's Lost Boys, who had been keeping me company with their thoughts of never wanting to grow up, were gone.

My husband was still intent on sweeping his numbers into long columns and catching their sum into a final mathematical dustbin. I proposed to him my need to peruse a pharmacy for some over-the-counter medicine with the other things we needed to do upon arriving. I used an "it's not a problem" tone of voice. Jeremy's countersuggestion was a North Hollywood emergency clinic.

I saw the smog as one dirty yellow tomcat asleep over the Los Angeles skyline.

Jeremy refused my request to drop me off at the emergency room clinic. He was adamant on accompanying me. I tried to move him to the right or left by stating the excessive time loss in waiting rooms.

"Let me call you at the office instead."

We sat together reading the old magazines. It wasn't fear, but merely a sadness that after only seven days of being Mrs. Foster I had to hear my new name uttered first by a nurse holding my forms at the corridor door.

I sat dangling my legs off the examination table. My sunburn was accentuated by the white kimono. It was that solitary wait for either the nurse or the physician to return with some word. A Hodgkin's relapse seemed unlikely, but it had also seemed impossible to me when first charted, and again at its recurrence. Old statistics rose up in my memory, both from medical magazines and from the mouths of past doctors. I remembered again the staff radiologist stating to his students that this patient cannot live long. He never knew how his statistics had filed teeth and wings that chased me.

I ached for Jeremy, waiting for me over two hours in the outer public chamber. Maybe he's remembering counsel not to marry me because of my medical history. His face materialized on the inside of me, along with the children who somehow were visualized in their pajamas. The image of them flickered and was gone.

Illness is like night when it comes drawing itself out as darkness and covering one's whole world. But without a night, there would be little revelation of the universe.

"Not now," I cried.

It was an emergency prayer telegram. It was true to the form of being to the point in as few words as possible.

I have known of some "sighs" that were answered because they were directed at God.

I could tell it was the doctor's footsteps. They move directly, not with the reluctance of a patient.

"Well, you are sick. They found in the lab an enormous proliferation of white blood cells in your urine."

I remembered how chemotherapy could start a whole different kind of cancer, like leukemia.

"I want to start you on massive dosages of a sulfa component."

"You are talking about on an outpatient basis?"

The doctor looked puzzled.

"It's just a severe urinary-tract infection. It's important to finish all the antibiotics, even when the symptoms disappear."

I ran down the hall to Jeremy. Emotion was in every crevice of my face. I didn't need to tell him anything, as my countenance reflected the news. He enfolded my shoulder with his arm as we walked out into the afternoon sun. Our shadows were merged behind us as one figure with four legs.

November 1

"Now think, Laurel," said Jeremy, "how the name of a residential street rarely reflects the essence of the avenue. Melody Lane can be the entrance to the city dump. Towering Oak Drive doesn't even have to have a tree."

I agreed that Valley View wasn't a title that merely conjured an image, but was in every way appropriate. There was no section of the road that wasn't laid over a steep incline, giving view to a deep bowl.

The random houses were perched like birds on a

tree whose limbs twisted up into the sky. They weren't my familiar two-story pigeons of Portland streets, but these had exotic architectural plumage.

Clicking off the digits of addresses, I wanted to determine how close we were to our new home. I was in a frenzy of anticipation. I had slid to the front of the car seat and was urging Jeremy to use more speed than caution on the road's narrow turns.

I felt as if every recorded yearning to reside in a house with a husband was bursting forth from my mind's long storage. For years each conscious thought had been delivered to a cell and sealed by a bar inscribed "Not Yet." The recent sighs were familiar, but many emerging recollections had been forgotten. Among those was the memory of myself as a child wrapped in a white sheet, balancing on the arm of a chair. The perch was envisioned as an elephant in my marriage procession to a palace gate.

Once I saw it, I shouted an exclamation of delight which was more a sound than a word. The stucco siding and tile roof were Spanish. There was a mass of flowering vines that led to the front door. A cactus grew in a bed between the walk and drive.

I didn't throw a bridal bouquet, wear a blue garter, and neither did we even think of carrying me over a threshold. Instead, I shook my hand as if the gesture would help Jeremy be more limber in fitting the right key to the lock.

Once in the entrance hall, I surveyed a solid wall of empty bookshelves that was the backdrop to a staircase that flowed down in a dramatic width from where we were standing. At our side was another short flight that went up to a closed door.

"There are five levels," said Jeremy. Because he

lifted up his hand with the announcement, I envisioned rooms built on outstretched fingers, each at a different height in the air. Only furniture was needed to be their rings and nailpolish.

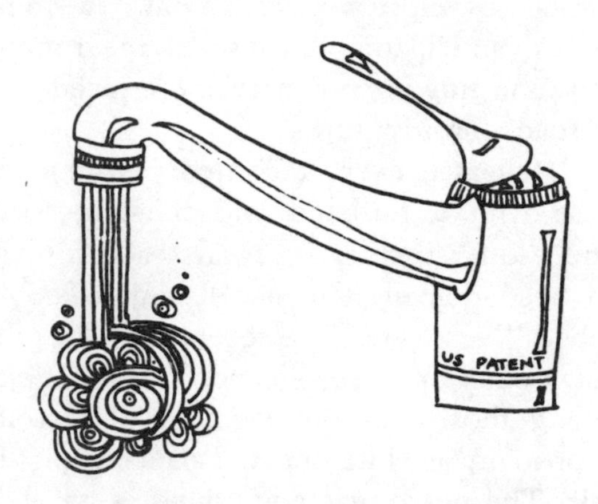

It was the kitchen at the bottom of the stairs that I liked best. The ceiling was crossed with the kind of hewn beams found in old cabins. I went and sat on the window seat, measuring from memory my number of antique cans to the length of oak shelves at the back wall.

Lost in the galaxies of pending decoration, I enumerated my varieties of dried flowers that I wanted to suspend with bunches of herbs.

"What?" said Jeremy. "I don't want any dead plants hanging from any ceiling."

Surprised, I stood up and said nothing more about interiors. Slipping my arm into his I looked out of the window to the meadow at the base of our hill. A large flock of goats was in view resembling an illustration from a children's book. One man stood in the midst of them holding a shepherd's crook. The animals all had their necks bent in grazing the wild grass.

"I love it here," I cried, "and you."

November 7

I was irritable. All the straight lines that form my logic were somehow being drawn into angles and corkscrews. I hadn't woken up that way. Some early morning thought had concealed in its folds a kind of black marking pen that was now shading all my perceptions.

Jeremy knew it. We stood in the backyard looking out at the hills and not at each other. I marveled at how we were learning to read the language of the other's face. One could translate the wrinkles at eyes, and decipher a lip's compressions.

I felt I should offer an explanation as a disguised apology. I had thought of several, of which he could select one, or combine a number of them together. I thought of my course of antibiotics, which was almost completed.

"I think being grumpy is a side effect from that regime of sulfa."

Jeremy is a kind man. It always seemed to be in the air surrounding him, but he listened without a comment.

I proposed a theory of conduct that I called "Newton's law of behavior."

"What goes up has to come down. It's the principle of emotional gravity."

I thrust both my hands into my denim skirt pockets.

"All that energy of preparing for the move and the wedding had to eclipse from that full-moon strength to this crescent. It's my own cycle."

It was a way that we were different. I had a tendency to emotional highs where I could be in the flight pattern of birds, or conversely request the moles to move over to make room for me.

My husband rarely flew or knew caverns. He was a straight line. We had gone through the house again together that morning, maneuvering around piles of cardboard boxes that needed to be unpacked. The larger pieces of furniture had been lowered into temporary locations given in haste to the moving men.

We each had our own proposals of what needed to be done to the home. My plan of priorities was perceived by Jeremy as ideas that challenged his, like a knight with a jousting stick. My language choice caused him to buckle his concepts in armor. The issue had been the living room paneling. I stood remembering with regret my sentences and exaggerated gestures.

"Jeremy, it's the very slickness of the walls that I object to. It doesn't imitate wood at all, but kitchen counters."

I went on to mimic chopping onions on a space above the chair. My experiences in remodeling old rooms had given me the knowledge to cover the plastic paneling in the living room with stucco.

Somewhere deep inside, Jeremy had closed himself to me, leaving me to imagine the damage I had done. He reminded me of a sensitive fern whose leaves fold together when touched.

Now we looked out at the California hills, bleached until they resembled cantaloupe skins in the distance. There were no goats or other animals to be seen in the meadow landscape. I was wishing our heads were set on one side with hinges so they could be opened and allow a fresh breeze to stir through the coils of brain matter.

I wondered briefly just how much of a mistake it was that we had never experienced being cross with each other before marriage. One thousand hours of telephone talk had never revealed our conduct when irritated. I wanted to analyze every detail while Jeremy was practicing a silence that now reminded me of venetian blinds tilted to an angle where no one could look in.

"It's the children too," I offered. "I miss them, and am glad they are coming in this week."

My husband drew me over to his side. The gesture and the weight of his arm absorbed my feeling of being upset. Somewhere back in my stored-memory panels was a flicker. It was the times long ago when I felt the same state of being out of adjustment, and unsettled by every puff of air. I remembered that it had turned out to be the opening weeks of my pregnancies. The memory was like an apparition created by see-through gauze. Half of me jeered: "Don't pay any attention to that ghost. You can't be pregnant. It's almost medically impossible. Only teenage unwed mothers conceive immediately."

The other side retorted: "The doctor said it could happen. You have had a lot of unusual and symptomatic nausea."

Jeremy lifted his face up to the sun to catch some more heat and color, before speaking.

"This is the first time that you are going to live without a cloud in the sky."

November 10

To drive Topanga Canyon's single road, one is putting pressure on either the right hand or the left to navigate the continual turns.

I had seen the simple wooden sign from the car window advertising the goats in uneven capital letters. It read "Milk and Fire Preventing Brush Removal" over a local phone number. I was becoming familiar with a number of highway landmarks. A trailer parked behind the one gas station was a dry-cleaning business. Close to the creek was a house with a life-size plastic cow set in the yard to face the highway. Hitchhikers used the road freely as one of the passages to the sea. Many of them had either a dog or a surfboard in tow.

Sitting next to Jeremy, I could feel a kind of nausea that would be produced if I had been doing somersaults in the back seat, or attempting to read a foreign language in small print. I knew something with my body was chemically amiss. The question of pregnancy could be answered by bringing a urine sample to a lab. Leaning back in the seat, I readjusted the weight of my body. We were driving to the airport to get the children from their late afternoon flight arriving from the Northwest.

The abnormal queasiness prompted me to ask one question in a way that was as casual as adjusting the sun visor:

"What would you think if I really were pregnant?"

Jeremy didn't laugh. He responded with the kind of reflex sigh that fills the lungs with enough air to visibly expand the chest.

"Laurel, you know I don't want more domestic responsibility."

Like Jeremy, my own season had passed of wanting another child.

Long ago, we had laid out the pattern of our marriage on the floor. We had waited for the date to pin it to the fabric of being together. The style of our garment was tailored to be that of companions, not where the woman functions exclusively as "mother."

Even without a further comment from Jeremy, I knew he had to be puzzling my question. I felt his thoughts reflected in a sideways glance.

"No," I responded. "I'm not talking about me wanting to get pregnant, just if it happened."

Jeremy answered my probe in a voice that lacked all enthusiasm.

"You paint a room pink or blue . . ."

Emotional subjects need to be neutralized with discussions of weather or politics. I proposed that the mayor of Los Angeles has a switch in his office for turning on the sunshine in the morning. The duplication of warm weather seemed almost mass-produced and artificial.

It was Anna who first spotted us in the airport lounge. She broke rank from the flight attendant and ran with a small hiking knapsack knocking against her shoulder. Her permanent teeth looked large in what was still a small girl's face. Matthew and Mary Elisabeth followed in a burst for first place, turning us into the finish line. There was a blur of small, new details. Matthew seemed taller and Mary Elisabeth's legs had a number of Band-Aids.

Jeremy was "Dad." They must have been practicing the word in their minds, as it came out alone and not in a stammer with his name. After we had stowed the luggage in the trunk, Mary Elisabeth leaned out in the space between us to again touch her new father. Jeremy had just adjusted his seat up closer to the steering wheel to give the children more room. The four-year-old first put her hand on his shoulder, sliding it down his arm to his stomach. She patted it and turned to observe to her brother and sister:

"It's just like a water bed!"

Once the children were in their new rooms for the night, the floor of my mind began to clear for a kind of internal pacing that I needed to do before sleep. Unlike me, Jeremy only needed to pull some television dialogue up to his neck. It's a sound for him that acts as a pillow to his ear. I waited until he was sleeping and deaf before rising to press every button in the room to make it dark and quiet.

I wanted to think about how we were each taking our places in the home we were beginning. The sense of contentment spread over my fears. "I wouldn't even mind being pregnant," I thought.

A kind of simplicity filled me. My mind began to feel like the single creator of all wedding card verses. Every rhyme invoking a blessing of unity was mine. I tried to scrape away the gold and silver curls of words to one idea of marriage: to maintain a commitment to the other's well-being.

A sleepiness began to bend my poems farther apart until I was finally without a syllable.

November 11

I only opened my eyes. The sky was the same rosy hue that resembles an Easter egg when it is first lifted from its cup of dye. The pink wash was beginning to be bathed in blue. I wondered if it was the color of dawn that prompted the tradition of dressing newborns in these same pastels.

Once I remembered my promise to show the children Topanga Canyon, I rose up on my elbow. My movement seemed tied to my husband. He rolled on his side and began to grab for some of the loose pillows that had been knocked against the wall in our sleep. Every morning was a new configuration of feather and foam pillows sculpted by our random tossings.

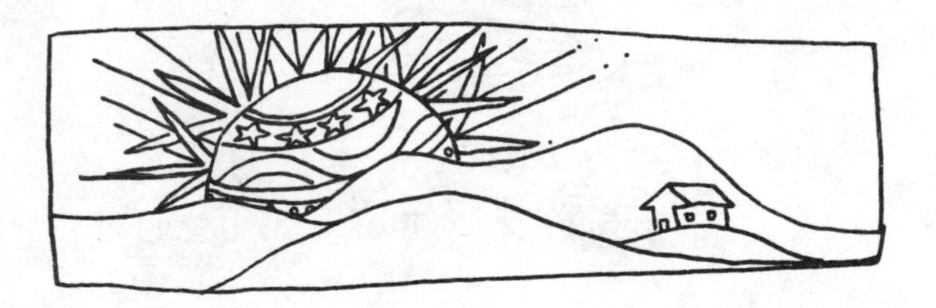

The children had lost the ability to walk in a house and talk in any tones other than the decibels that strenuously vibrate tonsils. Once they were dressed, I sent them to the car while I went to fish out an old radio microphone head from one of Jeremy's storage boxes. I had decided to imitate the monotone professionalism of a tour guide.

In the front seat I spoke into the microphone. It was the size of a golf ball on a stalk.

"Coyotes abound in these coastal range mountains, along with other small animal species. The size of a dog, they run in packs and can often be heard throughout the night."

While Matthew pronounced that was "cool," Anna began to imitate the coyote's high-pitched yelp. Mary

Elisabeth scanned the roadside demanding one to come into her view.

Because of the steep angle of the access road to our property the foot brake had to be pressed all the way down to the highway. We passed the one house that was posted with several signs stating that the residents paid a patrol service for professional surveillance. The phrase "Protected by Westinghouse" formed the upper message, and a different colored sign attached below read "Armed Response." I knew not to mention it to the children or the car would be filled with their popping sounds for imitating guns.

"I want you to note that the junction of our street with the main road is marked by that small health-food store out your right window." I had never entered it without finding customers that looked ready for a costume party.

Matthew deciphered, "Freshly squeezed carrot juice" and "We have DMSO" for his sisters.

I interrupted his letter "O" with instructions.

"To reach the elementary school, you will be passing this post office." I told them about the cat named "Zipcode" that lives under the counter.

Since they were going to be walking to school, I wanted to underline their route and get their enrollment forms. Matthew groaned when I turned up a steep hill labeled "School Road." He was already measuring his future exertions.

The Topanga Elementary School duplicated a kind of motel in its architectural layout, complete with having its office in the front. The secretary was fitting a plastic lid onto a lunch container as I ushered the children in for enrollment forms. Her appearance looked to me as if she could be valuable to birds, if only she would eat outside. Select crumbs, sized to fit a beak, had landed on her lap and the shelf of her bosom. Even her straw purse was unraveling, leaving long, pliable fibers that could line nests.

Anna answered her question that she was transferring from a Portland school.

"We're not going to live by the volcano anymore."

"That reminds me," said the receptionist as she pulled out more forms from a file cabinet. "You'll need to fill out the catastrophe forms with the children's emergency name cards."

The specific paper was on top of all the other information sheets.

> Topanga residents have been through enough calamities to know that disaster is a way of life in the Canyon and that *fire* and *flood* and *land movement* are probably inevitable.

My mind substituted the correct synonym, "earthquake."

> An emergency tag has been developed which will be used when the Topanga school pupils have to be evacuated. It will be fitted to the child's arm and should be filled out with all the necessary emergency information. The time to complete it is now. Delay is a luxury we cannot afford."
>
> HERBERT MINKER
> PRINCIPAL

I looked up wondering if the enumerated dangers were being exaggerated. I noticed the crumbs that had been attached to the receptionist person were gone. I spotted them on the clay tiles between her chair and cabinet. She's a friend to the small scavenger insect, I thought.

A short man opened an office door at the corner of

the room. Above the doorframe was a brass plaque inscribed, "Principal." Below it was a simple paper sign recording his Zodiac birth month symbol.

"I'm Mr. Minker," he said, eyeing the children.

"We do have a dress code at this school. All the students must wear shoes."

Since we were all properly shod before him, I thought he might be detecting certain latent tendencies.

"Have you told them about the rattlesnakes?"

"Just about coyotes," replied Matthew.

"We have a lot of them in this area, and the children should freeze, not bolt, when they hear one.

"Oh," he added. "Having just moved here, you're going to need an official identification card for access into the canyon when the road is closed."

I almost decided he was crazy, a candidate for the mad court of the queen in *Alice in Wonderland.*

Should we paint the roses red
While the earth quakes, rattlers shake
And calamities knock us all dead?

Instead, I declared, "I don't know what you are talking about."

He sent the secretary back to the file to bring out a paper typed on both sides. The title was centered in two lines and underlined.

OFFICIAL POLICY FOR ACCESS TO TOPANGA CANYON
DURING EMERGENCY SITUATIONS

I read that the California Highway Patrol has set roadblocks in the past forbidding all traffic except for those with the Topanga zip code on their driver's license. Those residents without the 90290 numerals have to get a special identification card. In parentheses it stated that it was renewable at a fee.

"Last year," said Mr. Minker, "were flooding and mudslides which washed out the road along with a number of residences."

Behind Minker was his office door. I noticed a small cartoon taped to its surface at an angle. It showed a man with a swirling mustache behind a desk. He was clad in a striped shirt, and there were three containers for papers in front of him. The labels on two of them read, "IN" and "OUT." The third simply said, "WAY OUT," and I directed the children back to the car.

November 15

I stood in the kitchen listening to the sound of morning. Even through closed windows I could hear the birds. Some pitched tonal patterns through small beaks, while others seemed to be doing imitations of rubber squeeze toys. Turning from the glass, I filled the kettle under the hot water tap. I compared brewing my husband's coffee to raising the American flag. There was a certain comfort in executing a now-established routine. The familiar red tin was on the second shelf flanked by cereal boxes. As my fingers lifted the five-pound can, a pain seemed to twist my spine into a small knot just below my waist.

Instinctively, I made a fist to press against it in order to alleviate its intensity by pressure. I froze, with my mind suspended from all thoughts other than a willing of myself to be normal. It was almost as if I hovered over my whole cellular structure asking for relief. As the pain subsided, I cautiously reached up for the porcelain pot and coffee filters. I made the toast with greater freedom, increasing my range of movements. Whatever wheel within me that had suffered the stabbing blowout, now seemed patched. I took the breakfast tray up to our room, holding it close to minimize the pressure on my back. Nonetheless, I decided to call a staff member at the University of Oregon medical school and have him recommend a Los Angeles doctor.

Seeing the coffee, Jeremy moved from lying on his side to leaning against the back wall. He had turned on the early news. His eye went from the tray back to the screen. Still feeling a throbbing in my lower spine, I wanted to share with him what just had happened. I looked at my husband closely. Jeremy's attention was swept into the graphs and clips of the New York newsroom. I decided not to worry him first thing as there were no absolutes until an examination. I knew Jeremy had been wrestling with his own production company problems which were requiring him to work until late at night, besides weekends.

After the office and school had claimed most of the members of the house, I searched for my Oregon clinic card. I found it in the bathroom drawer filed by the side of old and half-used medicines in a box. I read through the list of access numbers. Some sounded as familiar as old names in small print.

The radiation department receptionist put me directly through to Dr. Moss, the radiology chief of staff. I gave him only the thinnest sweet coating of news before the unpalatable substance of my question.

"Could you recommend a Los Angeles doctor as I've been suffering some unusual symptoms?"

"Repner," he replied, "at the City of Hope."

I knew it was the hospital that specialized in serious illnesses on a physician referral basis. I thanked him for making the necessary calls for getting me an appointment. Not knowing the answers about my health was becoming more painful than hearing the possible facts. Stress can produce a kind of rumbling in the pit of my stomach. It's a restless creature with a switching claw. Worry operates its retractable talons.

Still holding the phone on my lap, I sat on the bed wanting to call Jeremy. Even while dialing his office, I argued that he'll be in a conference or on a long distance line. Instead, the receptionist put me directly through. Jeremy never says, "Hello," but instead states his last name in a tone that implies, "State your business."

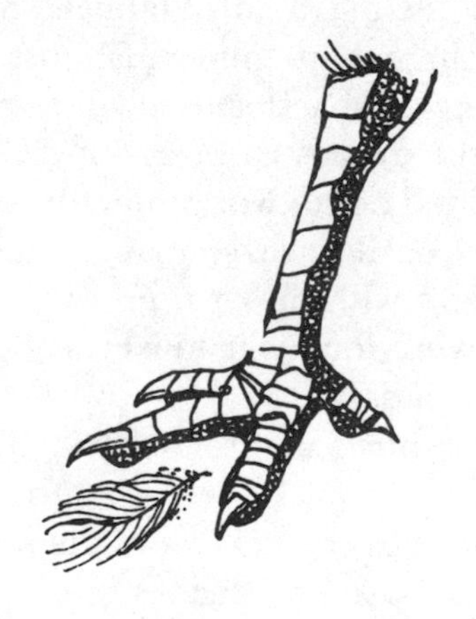

Not wanting to alarm him yet needing to communicate the facts made me relate my information in a way that sounded slightly insane.

"Something's wrong, but it's all right," I said.

My excessive use of a visual image further garbled

my message. I described the backache as a lead horse nudging through the other flying hoofs of unusual discomforts. Jeremy's questions pierced to the issue of the nausea and recurring lower back pain.

He said, "Go to the doctor, Laurel, and do whatever you have to do."

December 1

Mary Elisabeth stood on the driveway waving. After turning from her four last-minute hugs that had concentrated on squeezing my upper forearm, I could still see her framed in the rearview mirror. She had on one of Matthew's sweaters whose sleeve flapped at her wrist in the vigor of her farewell. Her visible affection made me feel like weeping.

Maybe it was because of the mirror's miniature proportions with her image converted to my forward view that made her remind me of a film clip. It was an old Sunday night insurance commercial that had rolled a progression of shots of a child growing up. It took the advertiser three minutes to move from a baby's first step through to the tossing of her graduation tassel. I knew it was my hospital destination that was casting the cosmic edge to my perception.

Next to me on the front seat was Jeremy's list of directions of freeways and exits to the City of Hope Hospital. Since he couldn't come to the appointment, I decided his absence would give me the freedom for visible lamenting. I already felt that my dashboard could become a wailing wall.

I pulled into the entrance of Ventura's four lanes, where all the cars were exceeding the speed limit. The automobiles only drop their acceleration to conform to the law when a police vehicle merges among the traffic flow. The mass of them reminded me of a school class that is instantly quiet when the absent teacher returns.

On the leash of my will, I brought out pleasant thoughts, like soft creatures for my mind to pet. In moments they bristled and bared their teeth.

"Stop it," I said. "Remember after the stage four diagnosis how a staff member wrote in your chart, 'We don't have much time left with this patient.' And here you are, years later . . ."

A certain perceptual intensity had me in its grip. The palm trees turned to silhouettes against the sky. What I saw was passing away, as if its location in time and space was so temporary that my eyes could render it transparent.

Maybe the process of dying, I thought, is like being blindfolded at a party. All the games have stopped so this one can begin. After a spin, there is only one tail to pin on the donkey.

"There is that which I cannot see, which will exist forever."

The hospital was far enough out of town to have

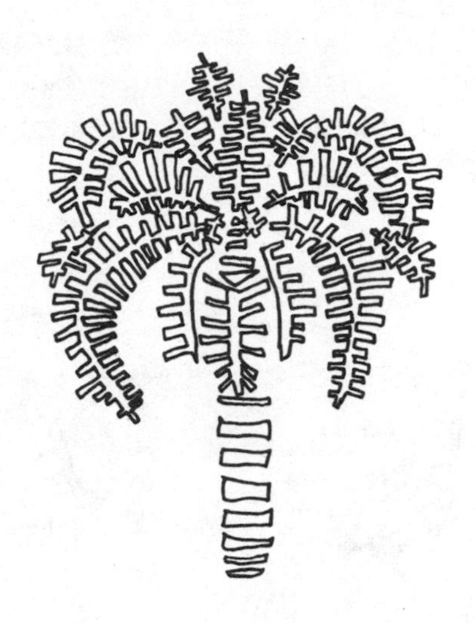

grounds that approximated airport runways for their length and sweep of lawns. From the parking lot, I could see a cluster of adobe-colored buildings. Their flat roofs testified to a climate that doesn't require drainage angles.

The entrance vestibule was blocked with three accounting and insurance desks. I passed through after asking for instructions to find the lunch room where I could wait my hour before the appointment.

Carrying my trapezoid-shaped cafeteria tray into the larger hall, my eye was struck by the simple plastic chairs. Every one had a plaque attached to its back with the name of its donor. There were hundreds of black signs on orange seats. Holding my beverage, I refused to sit in any place inscribed, "In Memory Of . . ." I found uncles and mothers and wives who gave chairs. My search for a seat reminded me that I had revived the juvenile selection process of choosing a horse among those at the carousel.

I picked
"DONNA VAN CAMP
HONORED BY HER
1973 FOOD SERVICE
CO-WORKERS"

Next to
"COME RAIN OR SHINE
THE CITY OF HOPE IS MINE
SAYS MOLLY T. WURTZLE."

After meeting the chairs, I saw that everything was bequeathed by donors. There were flower bushes and walls set with individual tiles for the small budget. Whole hospital wings and clinics were given by the rich. To find my way to the radiation department, I went through the Evelyn and Hans Kosterliz lobby to the Abe Silverman patient lounge.

My examination room reminded me in its size and sterility of a new tract-house bathroom. The counter by the sink held swabs and sticks, besides the shiny tools that give access to the body's interior. I took off my clothes so the white gown and my own flesh could blend with the opaque walls and carpeting.

Dr. Repner had a beard. That, with his hair, gave the impression that he would prefer to cover his whole face.

Even his eyebrows cooperated in looking like rolled-up shades that could be dropped over his eyes. While he pressed for any swollen lymph nodes, I studied the acoustic ceiling tiles, the rectangular neon light, and single water sprinklers. My bare feet dangled from the table and grew cold.

Knowing he would schedule X rays, I said, "There's a chance I'm pregnant."

"I doubt it," he replied, "but we'll check that first."

In the hematology lab, a call came for me to continue to the X-ray department. The instruction was so brief and impersonal that it almost sounded like a fragment of a sentence. I had been ready with my symptoms, and the one possible cause of pregnancy was ruled out by the technician's message. Relapse was the only other thing I knew that could make me so consistently ill.

Down every corridor were people who were very sick. They were being wheeled in chairs, resting on couches, or leaning on someone's arm. Illness has its own kind of marathon. Everything in me wanted to stop these miles of track, besides wondering where the finish line lay. I couldn't keep myself from wishing that Jeremy had arranged his schedule to come.

Walking into Repner's office, I decided it would take an effort to like him, only because he never seemed able to smile. He emitted a dark intensity. Behind him was a bookcase whose texts were names of cancers: *Brain Metastasis, Bronchial Carcinoma.* He had some pottery jars on the shelves between the titles. Inscribed in the clay by a potter were the words "Heavy Signs." The container on the top shelf read, "The original can of worms." It made me think that the history of medicine is a story of amazing intelligence and amazing foolishness.

He snapped an X ray up on a fluorescence-lit panel to his right.

"The lungs are clear, but . . ." He put a lower spinal cord X ray in its place. "See that evident damage on the fourth lumbar vertebra."

I sat there pretending that I could read X rays, but my only experience with the posture of bones was from Halloween skeleton decorations.

He used a pen to point at the white edges in the black field.

"It's right here in the cortical border. This deterioration is from the old tumor."

The moment seemed to stretch time to incalculable lengths in the pauses between his sentences.

"You must have strained this area. Have you been doing a lot of heavy lifting?"

"Lots," I said, thinking about the moving boxes.

"Then that's your problem, and all the nausea is just in association with that trauma."

Life and death are in the power of the tongue. I wanted instantly to be outside where I could see the sky. I took his phrase, "No evidence of relapse," and thought it should be carved on a plaque and fitted to a dining room chair. Dr. Repner still couldn't smile, but I did, out through the lounge to a pay phone.

The receptionist could only relate that Mr. Foster was out of the office at a meeting, and she was without a number to reach him.

While clearing the children's supper from the table, the phone finally rang. I ran upstairs to the extension while Anna began listing for her stepfather the elements of the dinner.

It seemed fitting that I should summarize all the medical conclusions standing up. If there had been any positive signs of illness, I would have thrown myself on the bed to be in a prone position while relating the doctor's assessment.

The moment seemed to be the landing of that invisible coin "Heads, she's up and well," and "Tails, down and sick." I had made myself dizzy watching it spin. I had kept trying to read "In God We Trust," engraved in the small print of the circumstance.

December 24

I stood in the kitchen stirring the cheese soup that would be our first course for Christmas Eve dinner. I made patterns with the spoon by first scraping figure eights against the copper bottom of the pan. Next, I wrote the alphabet in large letters as if to amuse my hand and keep it from quitting in the monotony of its task. One impulse seemed marked by my hilarity. I wanted to dye half the bowls red and the other half green, except, I paused, we were having company. I could count on someone associating my servings as derivations of catsup and disinfectant.

It was good to have Jeremy home. He was upstairs in our bedroom watching the news. It was the earliest he had ever been able to get away from the office. I thought about us in an image of standing at the edge of a snowy field and planning together the kind of tracks to carve. Jeremy and I had talked of inviting many people to come and eat with us. Tonight was one foot in the snow.

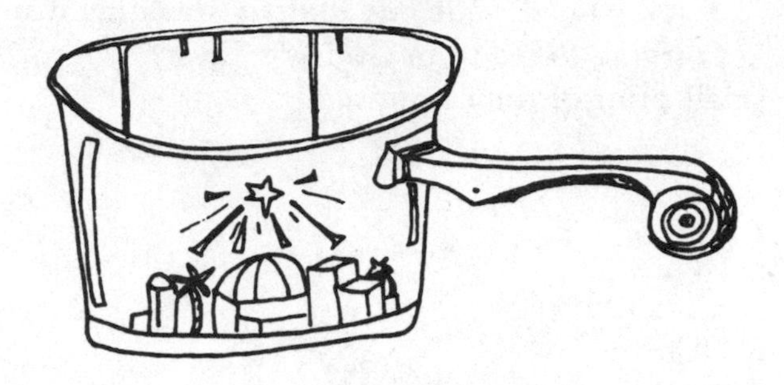

Our guests were due to arrive within the hour. Dr. Jean LaCour lived across the street; my door faced her door. She taught social sciences in a state university. I had never been into her house without finding a different configuration of textbooks on her rug.

It was Matthew who met the goat shepherd and asked him to come. He had found him while exploring back trails on his way home from school. He had described Gus McFadden to me as a bearded man standing in the midst of three hundred animals. Dogs were following his commands and running around the circumference of the herd. Matthew accepted the invitation to join them in their walk to the winter pasture that proved to be directly below our house.

I never knew which wall concealed the doorbell. It had a power in its chime to penetrate all five architectural levels. I could hear my husband invite Jean LaCour in.

Our neighbor looked as if she had dressed for the night in the back of an art gallery. Her jewelry was from a display case of bent wires soldered to pins. Her clothes were the vivid hue of oil paints when squeezed from the tube to the palette. I had observed that the average Los Angeles woman in her fifties weighs fifteen pounds less than a counterpart matron in Portland. It was an earmark of living in a city where one didn't wear a coat.

Jean took a chair over by the girls who were picking out walnut bits from a basket on the hearth. Jeremy put another log on the fire.

It was Matthew who saw the flashlight first in the backyard. I walked with my son down the stairs to the kitchen door marveling that our other guest had climbed up the steep brush trails to our deck.

The shepherd stood smiling. While shaking his hand I noticed he was missing one of his canine teeth. His countenance was the hardy health of those who work at jobs outside. His dark green pants were once part of some regiment officer's uniform. Now they had hay and bits of branch twigs embedded in the wool. He washed his hands in the sink while asking if this was really the right night. A faint odor of goat cheese mingled with the warmth of the kitchen.

Jeremy seated us at the table. The world has grown old while generations of fathers have pointed children to their right chairs.

Gus McFadden talked through the meal about his profession. He had a contract with the State of California for his herd to graze the firebreaks along the rim of the Santa Monica Mountains. Most of the months he roamed with his flock over a designated route, keeping it clear of all vegetation. He told us that he was the highest paid shepherd in history. Jeremy was interested in the wooden crook that he carried into the fields. Gus explained it was a tool that he laid over himself at night when sleeping in his canvas bag. One of its purposes was to provide visibility so the animals would not trample him if startled to flight by coyotes. As I got my platter of baked confections I could hear Anna ask to hear more about the canyon's rattlesnakes.

Once Dr. LaCour and Gus had left by doors at the opposite ends of the house, the five of us sat together watching the last of the fire's embers. My thought was to envision our years to come as pieces of fine furniture that time would arrange on its own carpet. No matter the length of the rug, I was sure it would be an intricate and well-woven destiny.

Jeremy interrupted my meditation by standing up to excuse himself. He wanted to go and watch the ten o'clock news upstairs.

"Stay with us," I protested. "Let a plane fall from the sky and a diplomat disappear without you knowing it."

He laughed while climbing up to our room. The sound of his humor acted as a shield that effectively blocked me from feeling hurt.

The children and I turned off all the lights except for those on the Christmas tree. We lay on the floor squinting, in order to blur our vision and alter the color patterns. Once the tree had the quality of Tokyo's neon, I explained to the children the story of the Christmas shepherds. It seemed to me that when the angels came with a message, the spokesman had to preface the formal announcement by saying to those in the field, "Fear not." Matthew paraphrased the sentence for his sisters as "Don't freak."

I thought through the next line,

"I bring you tidings of great joy which shall be to all people."

They seemed like words that could be embroidered on capes which, when worn, would confer the power of flight. I wanted our family to dress like that.

January 3, 1981

I chose a fresh carton for storing the Christmas decorations. It was my night's work to sweep us into January and

clean the hearth of candle wax. I folded away the children's wreath constructed entirely of breakfast cereal pasted on plywood. Some of the Cheerios had flaked off, but the outline of a bow in red Froot Loops was still intact.

I was in the grip of the kind of sentimentality that triples the weight of a heart. It made me yearn for a woman to talk to, as if sifting with another through feelings could diffuse my peculiar melancholy.

I turned over Anna's creation of Joseph to wrap in the L.A. *Times.* He resembled more a pizza crust struggling to stand upright, than a man. After closing the box flaps, I went into the kitchen and dialed the area code for Portland.

Once Arlene knew it was me, she was quickened with the facts of math.

"You've been married for two and one-half months!"

Her queries were without pause, as if each question mark was instantly swallowed by her next curiosity.

I said, "Yes," then spoke of the season. "The Christmas weather here is like a July picnic. Almost all of the store merchants paint their glass with snow scenes as they have to simulate winter."

Arlene replied that it had been raining, but Harlan and the children had gone into the woods to cut a tree anyway.

"I absolutely refused to pay the exorbitant price for fir trees on these L.A. lots after always chopping our own. So, I traded pans of cinnamon rolls for ours."

I confessed how I missed Oregon at odd times, like when I saw the winter coats at the back of the closet. It was the thought of losing the season's moment when one's hand first plunges into last year's winter pocket and by chance finds spare change or crinkled gloves.

"Are your children happy, Laurel?"

"Yes," I replied while shaking my head and forgetting that she couldn't see the gesture.

"How is Jeremy?"

"Fine. He works maximum hours with the energy of three men. I've told him that if he manufactured tires and was this absent, I couldn't bear it. So my encouragement lies in that I believe in the principles in his films."

"What exactly is his work?"

I had come to compare Jeremy's office to the surface of a stove.

"He has a number of movies for production that are in different stages of preparation. While some simmer at the back, another is boiling and needs to be constantly stirred. Scripts are only recipes."

I explained that Jeremy also does a lot of film distribution. "It's the process of organizing the number of places where a dish can be fed to viewers." I thought of theater seats as having the contours of a spoon.

"Are you ever sorry, Laurel?"

My mind instantly filled in the words that Arlene left out.

"Sorry . . . that I married?"

I started to quickly answer in a reply I would use to

everyone. The word "never" was at my tongue. But with Arlene, I had to pause.

"Sometimes I feel abandoned."

It seemed such a lack of loyalty to Jeremy to say it. Yet, I realized that the cause of my depression wasn't the end of Christmas, but his perpetual absence. I could feel my cheeks burn. The flush was more from my realization than from the statement I had made.

"Every couple . . ." said Arlene.

I finished her sentence for her. I knew her thought, her paragraph. It was the idea of marriage adaptations eventually providing more than a solid relationship, but maturity.

"I know, friend," I said. "Marriage is our best and last chance to grow up."

We both laughed, and I glimpsed a clubhouse where spouses sit behind the front lines to encourage each other.

Staring at the phone cord after hanging up, I felt like hearing the voice of other friends. I dialed another ten digits for long distance. Melanie's "Hello" made its journey through the coils and into my ear.

She had a question Arlene had never thought of. She asked about my work. It was one difference between the single mother and the wife that a husband supports. I told her I had no commitments for any public speaking. "But with Jeremy, I could go if I had to."

Melanie knew how I guarded that freedom even if I never used it.

I explained that my earlier activity had surrounded the event of being published and I had expected that professional part of my life to grow quiet in time. I was in a different season.

February 11

Climbing the stairs to our bedroom, I could hear the droning sportscaster calling out yard lines and plays. I had to hold the wood tray with Jeremy's coffee in one hand in order to turn the bedroom doorknob. Because of the carpet pile, my hip pressed the door only partway open. Jeremy had already read the Sunday paper, and now was watching afternoon football. Reclining on his side, he was engrossed by the electronic rectangle. The thought recurred that I had never known the breadth of televised athletics until my marriage. I was still incredulous that a reasonable, intelligent man could be thrilled by padded bodies slamming into each other looking for a ball.

I had tried to participate. I thought it was just a matter of knowing the rules in order to experience some level of enthusiasm. My small degree of cheering for one side would shift during a game to rooting for whichever team was losing. I felt that if football truly had some national women's audience, the commercials would include soap powders and use the team's soiled jerseys as a testimony to their cleaning power. Instead, burly men demonstrated aerosol foams for the camera's close-up lens.

I decided that my presence was comparable to the sacrifice of a woman staring with her spouse into the mechanical depths below the open hood of a car. I tried to explain my disinterest, reversing the circumstance for Jeremy.

"It's like a husband sorting through fabric bolts in order to look for bathroom curtain material that matches the tangerine toothbrush."

Looking over my husband's head, I could see the Santa Monica hills rolling by our horizon on the land's last stand before the Pacific. I had gotten used to views in our occupancy. Every window framed an expanse of sky. I would give up all indoor bathrooms and closets in order to keep vistas.

Jeremy called my attention back to the screen which continued to repeat the same slow-motion frames of a player intercepting a pass. It always made me feel like nudging the set as when a record needle sticks in a groove. I sat by him until it was over, then took my tray back to the kitchen. I could hear Anna's voice from the living room, correcting her sister's execution of a cartwheel.

"Then you do one!" retorted Mary Elisabeth.

I walked by them to the counter. The sink was full of dirty dishes, as I had spent the morning in church with Matthew and the girls. It seemed that the children's exclusive expression of hygiene was their habit of getting a clean cup for every sip of water. On the stove was a saucepan left by Matthew after heating himself a second bowl of soup. Between the pan and empty bowl were enough noodles that it looked like a message spelled out in some cryptic alphabet.

I needed to decipher a mystic's note. There seemed to be an emptiness to Sunday afternoon. It was a vague, restless feeling that I, alone, seemed to be experiencing. Everyone else in the house was occupied and content.

I fished the dishcloth out of the sink and squeezed out the old water from its last job. Opening the cupboard, I lifted out the liquid soap whose container was contoured by the manufacturer for a palm and fingers. The concentrate was dyed emerald green, and I squeezed twice what I needed into the faucet spray.

My negative mood was gathering strength. I felt disappointed that what I had yearned for seemed so dull. Part of me kept marveling that the clean bill of health didn't seem enough, whereas if I had been sick, it would have been. It was as though parts of my consciousness encircled me on bleachers and took seats to watch Laurel in the central arena.

There was a simple cheer from the good attitude: "Your life goal is not personal pleasure. Embrace the maturing that comes with any self-denial. . . ."

Its voice was quickly obliterated by passion. It brought a quote from literature. Elizabeth Barrett feared to take Robert Browning's hand in marriage because, she said: "In that first wedded year, the men always change from being the lover to a husband." I could feel my irritation that Jeremy's only expression of leisure in four months of marriage was to close himself away for the entire Sunday with the newspaper and sports.

"Stop," I said out loud. This was the epidemic of discontent. I decided that it resembled the bubonic plague of the Middle Ages in wiping out more families than history can number. What scared me was feeling the anger within myself. It couldn't be simply talked away with a couple of admonitions. With it was the knowledge that I could be extremely foolish instead of wise.

One woman plucks down her house, while the other builds it up.

Remembering that the thirteenth-century monks put

ashes on their head in repentance, I scooped our some suds and mashed them into my hairline. Beginning to feel better, I used both hands to cup more bubbles which I wiped onto my head, above my ears.

Give me the power
To be the person
I want to be.

Jeremy came into the kitchen. I knew it must be halftime and some coordinated bands were marching on a distant field. I stood by the tub of half-washed dishes with soggy hair and wet shoulders where the water had run down.

I anticipated him to react, in a smile or with questions. Instead, I don't think he even saw the soap as he registered no response at my appearance. He simply said that he wanted to make some popcorn. I started laughing, and in a single move, went and put my arms around Jeremy's neck. If there were still any devils hanging around whispering fiery accusations, our embrace made them flee. Jeremy went back upstairs, oblivious that I had known those thoughts that were like clouds, a storm, and then a calm.

March 17

After the children were asleep, I sat on my bed hoping to lose myself in some author's plot. But instead, I kept straining to hear Jeremy's motor in the sparse nighttime traffic. I sighed as every car kept climbing above our driveway.

"Laurel, you married an absolute workaholic."

It was a realization that had become increasingly clear. I had believed that our relationship would share a maximum of times together. It was one of my greatest expectations that I had wrapped around my pulse, beneath my bridal gown's satin sleeve. Our months together had slowly unwound that hope.

Snapping the book shut, I went out to stand on our bedroom's back deck. A neighbor's dog was barking in response to an animal's distant bay. I was beginning to really know Jeremy. The mysteries of each other were being solved by the quantity of days we were living together. "The future" was no longer one of our most widely spoken languages with its dialect of promises. I knew he had been sincere and meant his personal vows, but habits can be stronger than intentions. I sighed.

I always knew this hour comes to couples. It's that inevitable realization of how different two people who live together can be.

I had only glimpsed beforehand how Jeremy's desk and working papers were his real living room and warming hearth. With reluctance, he took his leave of them at night and rushed back to greet them at dawn. He had no concept of family time, or even the necessity of a meal together.

I thought of the Minnesota boy that was father to this man. He had been molded by the constant labor of an impoverished truck farm, while I, a child of the suburbs, had had time to lie on my back making stories for every fleet of clouds.

Another dog joined the sounds of the night. Somehow I felt my thoughts had a long, drawn-out barking quality to them, too. The facts that it was Saturday and after ten o'clock were against me. It was that time of weekend which removes one's defenses against loneliness, so it had begun its seepage under the bedroom door.

Returning to my room, I pulled back only the screen to allow for a maximum draft of cold air. I unlaced my tennis shoes and pulled them off. The upper seams had pressed small lines along the tops of my feet. While rubbing from my ankle across to my toes, I thought that there's an invisible baton passed from a first wife to a second for that long-distance run of a relationship. In Jeremy's long marriage to Patty, they had lived for intermittent years in separate residences. I could think of her now with real compassion for her unfaithfulness. She had had a husband who was never there.

Hearing a far-off motor already in second gear, I listened for its decision by our driveway. It drove on past. Its engine went whining by our neighbor's far row of poplar trees and up to its own summit.

Pulling open the bottom drawer, I decided on the flannel nightgown whose nap seemed polished from use. It had not been worn since Oregon nights. I wanted comfort in the yards of cotton. I knew that I would have to have a serious talk with Jeremy. The thought of a pending conference filled me with some uncertainty about how to approach him. He seemed to me like a powerful locomotive consumed by pressing forward with his ministry of movies.

"Jeremy," I practiced, "the only problem is the order in which you pull your cars behind you. Your family seems somewhere at the end of the line."

Maybe, I thought, I'm at the edge of adaptation and need to register my last complaints before forming whatever colors of skin it's going to take to make me blend with my environment.

Shutting off the larger light, I left for my husband the dimmest bulb lit over a three-inch sculpture of a man and woman's hands entwined.

April 10

It was morning. Jeremy stood at his chest of drawers in vapors of aftershave lotion that curled out from his neck into the atmosphere.

"Jeremy, you know the story of Old Testament Esther?"

"Yeah," he replied, turning to me with his day's choice of black socks in his hand.

"She went through elaborate preparations before telling her husband what was wrong with the kingdom. She fasted three days and then went to stand in the throne room before him. When he asked what she wanted, Esther held back the issue and asked him to a banquet of wine. She concluded the evening by inviting him the following night for the same refreshment, and then gave her message. Let's pretend I did all that, Jeremy."

I had his attention. He pulled out a chair and sat at the small oak table that had fluted legs like four stacks of pumpkins. His choice of seating provided conversational distance. I began to feel a deep inner nervousness that potential confrontations produced in me. It was my peculiar vulnerability. There is an old twinge of insecurity that strikes through my bones, like joints that ache in certain weather.

Yet, I was blunt.

"I need to see more of you. We need to see more of you."

"We, I," he replied in a kind of non-answer.

"The family has to be given more priority."

Jeremy stood up and started moving back to his dresser, reaching into the corner that held his handkerchiefs. He was going back to his occupation with dressing. I felt it as a dismissal. His silence made me join the hand of frustration to that of reason.

"I think in these past five months we've had three meals together as a family, two at Christmas and one at Thanksgiving."

It was a fact, not an exaggeration to make a point.

I was sorry, but not surprised, to see my feelings rise and the beginning ground swell of tears. In the past I had blamed his expense account, which opened for him every restaurant door without personal cost. I now knew it was deeper than that. An established behavior has a power developed through years to continue in its own momentum.

Jeremy's continuing silence set loose enemy soldiers that moved in rank from my thoughts to my mouth. They were the hosts of resentment, with each unit wanting to attack with its own accusation of his broken promises.

Jeremy was controlled. He didn't raise or quicken the tempo of his voice, yet there was an illusion that he shouted at me.

"Laurel, will you stop being so intense!"

I knew I was handling it wrong. I was throwing my message for help into the sea and had failed to get it into a glass bottle.

I walked over to the chair that Jeremy had vacated. I saw that my point of view had started through the labyrinth of communication, but lodged itself in some blind alley.

Jeremy sat down on the bed. It was as though our bodies were moving in a circle almost as a shadow to our thoughts.

"I used to think of you, Laurel, as being much more

professionally motivated than you really are. You don't travel and speak at all compared to what you did before marriage."

It was said to me with the slightest tone of reproach.

I had always feared that once married I would be guilty in a husband's tribunal because of my wanting to accept invitations. Now the hour of the issue had come and my censure lay in the fact that I received so few.

I looked out the window realizing that I had disappointed him too.

"Exactly what do you do during the day?"

His question was without sarcasm, and neither was it asked as a means to gather some defense for my charge of his absence. He simply seemed curious.

My impulse was to detail every stage of the scrubbing of carrots. Instead, I held up three fingers while making a list.

"Housework, nurturing the children, and I write in my diary."

Jeremy continued to look at my upraised hand while I answered. His voice was contemplative.

"You need more personal time. I want you to call an agency and start interviewing for a live-in housekeeper. Look for numbers in the want ad section under 'Domestics.' "

To him the issue was solved, and Jeremy walked to the closet to select a tie. He rolled the green silk strip into a knot. The pattern was of small, evenly spaced black whales.

I realized he was trying to provide for my needs by duplicating for me what he himself required. My heart softened. Maybe he was putting Band-Aids everywhere but on the sore, yet his evident affection seemed to be a far greater salve than his solution.

"Laurel, you can come down to Summertree Productions and write in a room at the office."

I nodded a quick assent while thinking how that would allow us more time in proximity. In addition, I reflected, it could be a quiet place to sit with words, turn them to beads, and string lines into my journal.

I followed my husband to the door. Holding his briefcase, he turned and kissed my cheek. The rear tire of the Mercedes drove over the daily paper that was folded in thirds and bound with a string.

April 16

Julia sat next to me on the front seat. I remembered to pronounce her name by saying first the single syllable "Who," according to the language of Central America. Each of her front teeth was framed in gold. It was a distinct style of dentistry where the enamel looked gift-wrapped. The agency counselor had just told me that my new household help was from El Salvador, and didn't speak any English. She, herself, had just learned of my lack of vocabulary. I could only ask her name, age, and the time.

I stopped at the large grocery by the intersection of Sunset Avenue and the Pacific Coast Highway. All shoppers can look to the water's horizon from the parking lot. Taking a cart, I read the dual advertisement embossed on plastic for a toddler's seat. Only in the Pacific Palisades is the Safeway store paid a fee to exhibit a phone number for a limousine service, and the address of a canyon nudist colony.

As Julia locked her door I thought how I knew nothing of her but what I could romance, a young woman who had escaped a war-torn country. I couldn't think of her as a maid, but more as a creative extension of the foreign exchange student service.

Julia didn't know it. Once through the electric door, she took the cart and held it back, intending to walk behind me at a servant's pace. When I slackened my speed so we could be abreast, she took half-steps to keep a few feet behind me.

I said, "Me, sister," and tapped the area one button down from my collar. It was futile. Her only response was to correct my name to its proper form, "Señora Foster," and take the can of stewed tomatoes from my left hand.

The market had the usual double parking in the vegetable section and along the row of cello-wrapped meats. Julia stood quietly at attention as I shuffled through the chops and links. I saw comments in other customers' eyes as she interceded to keep me from putting anything in the cart myself.

"Don't believe it," I wanted to protest to the eyebrows that lifted into the first wrinkle of a forehead. "This is not my style!"

In the checkout line, I thought of how I was now testing the other end of a continuum. Five years ago, I had had to hoist Matthew into the large grocery dumpsters that were located at the backs of stores where trucks parked for unloading. The child would place one foot on my interlocking palms in order to reach the fruits with two or more spots, plus the packages that lived on the shelf beyond their code date.

As Julia carried the bags to stow herself in the back seat, I wondered at this manifestation of another hand for my broom. I decided it was an opportunity to test a fantasy. There have been times when I have waded out into a dirty house, been up to my hips in chores, and wished for help.

I fished through my purse looking for my car keys, only to find the familiar bulge in my pocket. Julia climbed in beside me, and bent over to pick up some well-tread scraps of children's papers.

"Oh, Jeremy," I thought. "I'm looking forward to the office, but a maid and a new room can never be a solution."

While pulling out into the traffic I remembered my suspicion that the wind in major cities has more molecules of ambition than the air in Portland streets. Even if I wanted to please my husband, I knew I could never have Los Angeles lungs.

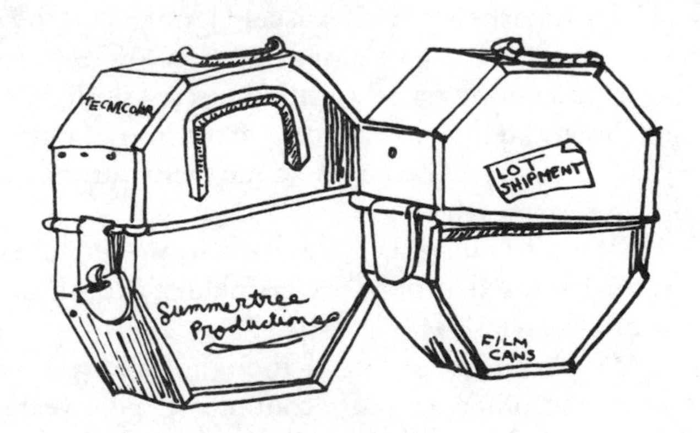

May 10

There was no sound or glow of light coming out into the hall from beneath Matthew's door. Over an hour had elapsed since I had positioned his blankets and heard his prayers. As I thought of it later, there was no real reason for me to have ever opened his door.

I found him looking straight up with the entire circumference of his cheeks wet from crying.

Quickly, I sat by him, asking what was wrong.

"Dad," he said. "I don't even feel like I have a dad. I never see him. He comes home after we're asleep, and when he is home, he just stays in the room and acts like it's his private motel."

While Matthew talked I remembered Jeremy's old promise to adopt the children. Yet I knew if their last name had been changed legally in court to "Foster," he still wouldn't be any different. I suspected that his conduct with my children was no different from how he had once related to his own.

I held him, but had to use my tough voice to speak Matthew's name. Self-pity is a lake, and I wanted to get my son back to shore. I've known its swells and depths.

With my arm around him, I asked, "If Jeremy were a blind man, would you expect him to go hiking or play sports with you?"

"No, but that's different!"

"There's all kinds of blindness, Matthew. He isn't meaning to hurt you at all. He just doesn't see."

"Okay, I'll try to believe that," he replied.

Once Matthew slept, I took my keys to drive to the Summertree Productions office. The lot seemed empty except for Jeremy's car parked in the stall closest to the street. His drawn curtains were the only rectangle of light at the front of the building. I knocked and waited for him to come and unbolt the door locks.

"Long distance," he said, and retreated back into his office. From the receptionist's desk I could see his backdrop of bookcases and filing cabinets.

Instantly I remembered his mother's apartment and her boxes of cloth scraps equal in amount to Jeremy's papers. I thought of him as a man engrossed in making quilts with some squares of scripts and others of contracts, held together with the fine stitching of promissory notes.

My assigned room was smaller and across from the accountant's office. From the door I could see the minute, glowing light indicating Jeremy's active line. I switched on the fluorescent overhead panel and sat at the old library table. My desk was littered with slogans of encouragement while my paragraphs of complaint were buried in my journal. At random, I opened to an old entry and read out loud:

Today we have been married six months. Sometimes I see these days as garments folded in half by noon, and rolled into the last quarter by nightfall. Our habits make them seem almost identical in fabric and design. But through the perspective of time, I'm beginning to feel that something is missing, as if there is a lost button, or a certain worn spot at the elbow.

Restless, I snapped the notebook shut and decided that the olive-green rug and white walls were in a plot together to oppress me. Seeing that Jeremy's phone light was still on, I wandered back to the warehouse where the computers and packing supplies were stored. Passing by desks, I noticed that their surfaces were empty, as if their keepers had to straighten them at night in counterpoint to making their beds in the morning.

The Xerox machine was emitting a low-powered hum. On an impulse, I raised the lid and laid the side of my face on the square where the papers were put for duplication. Pulling the cover back over me, I shut my eyes and punched the "One Copy" button. The machine shifted, carrying the weight of my head across the photographing light. The etching was deposited into a mesh basket. I examined the Xerox image of my skin folds and eyebrow hairs.

I thought, "After all the radiation treatments I've had, this can't hurt me," and began to experiment with degrees of pressure on different expressions.

I didn't know that one of the accountants was working. I straightened up and found him staring at the president's wife who had been photographing her flaring nostrils. He was a somber man, wore glasses, and had some lesions from what was once troubled teenage skin.

"It really works, Len."

I said this while showing him a sample from my series of photos.

"Try it," I urged.

Len first put his hand on the machine and the print duplicated his palm. Encouraged, he cast one look to make sure there were no spectators to his folly, then put his face flat on the machine. His glasses came out the best with the rest of him receding into darkness. He took his pictures with his briefcase and left by a back door.

I took a selection of my new art into Jeremy's office. He swiveled around and took them from me, smiling.

"These are wild."

"Conference," I said. "Topic: Matthew."

I was mimicking a business sheet by stating my agenda. It was a costume for my approach. If I cried, and was naked, Jeremy would be less apt to hear me.

"He wants more interaction with you. It's a deep need, as he hasn't had a father since the age of five."

I could feel the control in Jeremy's answer like a stick shift pulled back for a steep hill.

"You've got all the time you could want for him now, Laurel."

His reply was underlined by the tone, "That is your responsibility."

Ancient as caves is the rage of a mother bear who will stand in front of her cub to protect him. I wanted to shout, "You're making the same mistake with us as you did with your first family."

But instead, my reply had a slightly higher pitch: "People are more valuable than these unending projects."

"The office" and "the family" could each be a hilt in our two swords, raised and crossing each other in tension.

There we sat on brown upholstered chairs with wheels at the bottom of their legs. We were both thinking the same thought: "You just don't understand."

Following Jeremy's taillights back into Topanga Canyon, I talked to myself.

"Don't be dumb, kid. You're not ever going to string together the right words that are going to bring your husband enlightenment."

I knew one solution would be to squeeze out for myself drops of the same fortitude I had developed during the years of being alone with the children.

Deciding to compose an "Ode to Acceptance," I sang it to the street lights:

My husband is an astronaut,
He lives up on the moon.
It's too far out in space
For him to come home soon.

Once in the quiet black chamber of my side of the bed, I continued to be beset with stanzas. I thought of it as the "Ballad of Growing Up." With one eye sunk into the pillow and the other staring at the knob on the chest of drawers, I altered the tune to the lilt of an Irish jig:

The princess met Prince Charming,
They rode on his white horse.
But in every castle dungeon
Is some dragon of remorse.

September 3

Matthew was laughing. He held his hands to his shoulders, demonstrating for his sisters next to him in the back seat of the car how to play "Jello." It was a style of riding up the street where gravity alone directs the body's mass. No muscles or bones are allowed to be in operation. Three children rolled against the door while I turned into our driveway.

Anna heard the telephone first. I ran inside, counting the rings and shouting to Julia that I would get it.

Jeremy's greeting came through the phone receiver from his Minneapolis hotel room. He explained he had been in a lengthy conference with his ex-wife, Patty. They had been in the office of a state agency that counseled in family services.

"She is completely unable to cope with our youngest daughter, and is demanding that Jessie be sent back to Los Angeles to be in my custody."

"How long?" I asked, envisioning a carnival barker who guesses numbers. His tablet was blank, and as Jeremy replied, "Permanently," I saw the figure for infinity.

All that I knew of Jessie Kay Foster was that she had an established pattern of being a troubled youngster.

"There are two solutions. We could look for a well-regulated boarding school, or . . ."

I interrupted Jeremy, repelled at the idea of shuffling away any child with such apparent needs.

"No, let's give her a real home."

Even while saying it, I could feel my heart sink. Some offstage voice in my mind was whispering, "You're really in for it now." I decided it was the lead part from that chorus that chants at young parents, "Just wait until they become teenagers."

"Laurel, her older sister, Gloria, also wants to come out later and just be a help in any way she can. She has written away for a catalog of a college in Malibu."

The carnival barker was back with a new number on his slate. It read, "Age 25."

Jeremy detailed how the two of them could use the outdoor guest room. We had remodeled a tool closet, tripling its floor space, and added glass doors, plus a deck. A set of cedar stairs joined it to the main house. They could have the kitchen bathroom for their use.

I began to feel a kind of panic at such rapid, impending changes that Jeremy was suggesting for our home structure. I said the noble words, "I'll do my best," but my phrase was a corset, and I could feel the flesh squeezed and bulging around my intentions.

After hanging up the receiver I looked out the window at the dried bush of sage growing next to the straggling strawberry plants. My thought was that everyone in life is a coolie toting boxes on their head. I could feel a new weight being lowered through space toward my load.

Seattle, Washington, September 10

I carried my own suitcase while counting the hotel door numbers trying to match the digits to the key in my hand. I passed the alcove where machines dispensed ice, candy, and cigarettes. I liked the impersonal quiet of the corridor. No one was to be seen; only an occasional muffled television testified to occupants behind closed doors.

After securing the lock, I looked around, welcoming the deeper chamber of my room. The following morning I was due to appear as a luncheon speaker and then back to the airport for my return flight to Los Angeles. The sense of refuge made me sigh.

Sitting down at the desk chair, I preferred the seat to either the couch or bed. I had the impulse to write, but didn't want my diary. Instead, I opened the single drawer and took out two sheets of stationery.

It was my marriage I wanted to think about. I needed a clarity of perception, and hoped it would come in my night's distance from home. The surrounding streets of Seattle were about a thousand miles from my entrance hall. Turning over the hotel insignia, I stared at the blank pages before drawing a minus at the top of one sheet, and a plus on the other. This wasn't going to be the frivolity of my old lists wondering if a boy loved me or loved me not. My issue was no longer numbering daisy petals.

I printed under the sign of the plus:

1. *Husband has loving affection for wife.*

   After a pause, I added,

2. *Personal conviction that wedding vows are meant to be a permanent covenant.*

Somehow, I had first expected to detail the paper bearing the minus with single-spaced lines of complaint. I had wanted to denounce everything that had ever bothered me, including Jeremy's television and the trivial fact that he used two clean towels after every shower.

Instead, I traced over the minus with my pen, then wrote:

1. *Unexpected difficulty in forming new family identity.*
2. *As marriage partners, we have completely different perceptions of how the family's time, goods, and affection should be shared.*

I knew I had reduced it to far too simple terms.

Pushing back my papers, I stood up. I could hear rain. They still used sash windows when the hotel was constructed. I tugged the handle, finally wrenching the frame up and apart from layers of paint that had sealed it shut. The building's eaves only allowed the palm from my outstretched arm to get wet. I could see couples walking below me on the sidewalk.

I began thinking of relationships as a kind of color wheel. I put myself in the center surrounded by men who represented the infinite hues of the personality spectrum. My realization was that I would eventually clash with the peculiar faults of any husband's character. Everyone was tinted. During years of singleness I had deceived myself with fantasies of slick congeniality.

For Jeremy and me, matrimonial harmony was going to be a gradual process through years of applied effort.

I felt better. Even the thought of Jeremy's children coming didn't seem like a threat anymore. My brain had felt like a dull or broken pencil point that had needed to be sharpened.

September 20

The first passenger off the Northwestern flight from Minneapolis was a mother with her fragile infant wrapped in flannel. From her arm hung a diaper bag filled with samples of manufacturers' products in plastic; pants and bottle, toy and bib. Already, the businessmen were passing her by with briefcases scarred from taxicab doors.

Both Jeremy and I strained to see through the crowd for Jessie.

With apprehension, I thought of the recent telephone call relating that the child's behavior was still troubled. She had run away from home one more time.

"There she is!" said Jeremy, pointing to a statuesque girl who started waving. I realized I had been expecting the kind of teenager that lives in the corner of Greyhound bus stations. They ask for cigarettes and have visible tattoos.

Jessie Foster walked to her father and related an account of a fly in the coach section who would now find itself in Los Angeles. She raised her hands and told it entirely from the insect's point of view. I knew I would like her. She used certain expressions that showed intelligence.

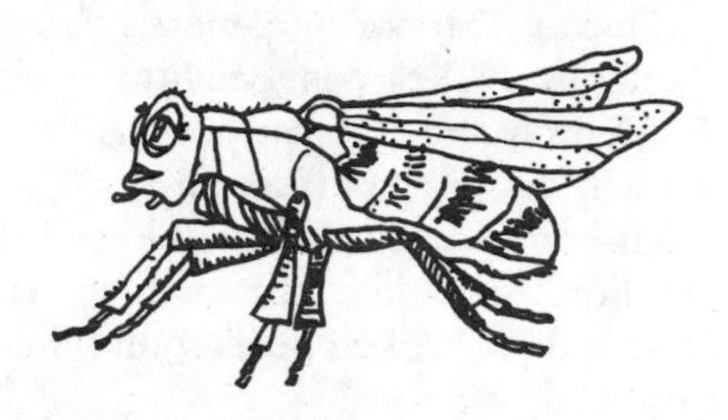

Jessie was dressed in a plaid blouse and skirt, the clothes of a department store school catalog. Her honey-colored hair was short. I could see her earlobes had been perforated for the potential of holding a number of pierced earrings.

Once in the canyon, Jeremy put his hand on my leg just as he bypassed our street, choosing other mountain roads. He looked at Jessie in the rearview mirror and said, "We're almost there."

I thought of it as a joke and decided he was searching through the back ways for a tumbledown cabin to pretend was ours.

It was as if he counted the exclamations from the back seat about our isolation before pulling into the drive.

While getting Jessie's boxes out of the trunk, Jeremy

whispered, "I want to suggest a confusing distance between our home and the main road."

Matthew and the girls rushed out of the front door. Their legs had turned to pogo sticks while shouting every sound of welcome. I knew inside were signs that they had colored for their greeting of a big sister. Anna had come to me with her crayons, asking how to spell "Jessie."

October 15

I looked at Jessie's radio on the kitchen window seat. It was an enormous box with a metal handle bolted to its frame. Two thermometers seemed to be pressed under glass. They were the numbers and degrees for AM and FM. All sounds that the radio amplified were primitive body rhythms. I punched the "off" button on the top while Jessie hung several pairs of wet Levis outside.

I watched my stepdaughter through the glass. She had taken shears and cut the bottom off her T-shirt. Her alterations gave room to three inches of exposed flesh between the garment and her waistband.

When she came inside, I handed her a bowl of frozen bananas that I had just processed in the blender. The

mixture had the texture and look of ice cream. We sat together at the oak table by the window. I didn't have Jessie's attention, but just an occasional nod from the outer orbit of her mind.

"I had always seen men hitchhiking. The first woman I ever saw soliciting a ride was myself."

Jessie stopped her ranges through space to stare at me.

"It was 1962. I convinced a girlfriend to join me. We stood at the curb feeling a personal offense at every car that passed us by."

"You were fifteen!" Jessie exclaimed.

Her surprised expression reminded me of the wonder common to retirement-home nurses when they look at the wedding pictures of their aged patients.

"Yes," I agreed, while suppressing my desire to laugh. "The same age you are."

Jessie's eyes took flight again. She traced a ceiling beam to her radio.

"I have a friend," she said hesitatingly. "My friend used to hitch rides. She was fourteen and pregnant. She lived in an unwed mother's home. My friend gave up a baby boy to a farm couple who could never have children."

Jessie's voice paused slightly between words. I watched her conclude by biting her bottom lip. Some gestures are richer than speech for meaning.

"It's more than I did, Jessie Foster, and no one knows; neither my parents nor friends."

I was the one who now looked away.

"It happened years before I asked Christ to forgive me and guide my life. My past, with its own secret, has formed the planks to my soapbox when I stand crying, 'Stop a worse slaughter in the seas than dolphins.' "

Our moment of communication made Jessie and me want to touch each other's hand, but we didn't. We both had more things to say, but we were quiet. No more gestures or speech were needed.

My thoughts flowed past the child to her father. I wanted to wire him a message:

One sentence to this letter,
Everything is better.

October 20

As Jeremy held open the restaurant door, my senses were first struck by the music whose notes gave me the images of girls who work in tea stalls, shuffling their feet, averting their eyes, and bowing. There was also a fish smell. From our entrance, looking beyond the simulated bales of rice, I could see a sushi bar.

I kept thinking, "We have been married one year tonight." I looked down at the new opal ring that Jeremy had just given me outside after parking the car. Once seated, my husband put his hand on my arm. It was as if a deposit had been made in that deep internal vault that needs romance. All displays of affection are its currency.

I had a thought about millions of couples over thousands of years. I spoke in general.

"Marriage provides the much-needed opportunity to surrender to something beyond one's own self-interest."

Jeremy looked up, having appraised my sentence as being specific and an initiation of a truth session.

"Still, Laurel, I'm not finding marriage as rewarding as I thought I would."

It was an acid retort to sentimentality. I wanted to respond with cynicism and pleas. Oh, Jeremy, maybe no one does, but say some sweet things tonight. I reflected how one difference between a good evening and one that is strained is to leave a few things unsaid. My speech reached down to talk about my dinner order.

Jeremy was deft with his chopsticks. No bamboo shoot was too slippery for his skill. After only spearing the denser vegetables, I abandoned mine for a fork. Jeremy's declaration of not being as content as his courtship anticipation had lodged in me. Even the fact that I repeated it again within myself was a signal of its damage.

I knew that during the year we had both had needs that cried like orphans left out in baskets by the other's door. No one had come to pick them up. Mine was the girl wanting to be cherished and included; his was the boy wanting to be admired, yet independent and free.

Jeremy brought up the topic of the children.

"Jessie sure seems to have stabilized. I think in part it's due to being shifted in position from the youngest and last at home, to the oldest and adored."

"I think she's extremely creative, Jeremy."

I had found her earlier this week in the kitchen with a game she had designed and mounted on cardboard. It was a symmetrical drawing of sunglasses sectioned into squares. She had inscribed it, "Punk in." The tokens progressed from conformity in the beginning, entitled "The Total Preppy," to punk culture.

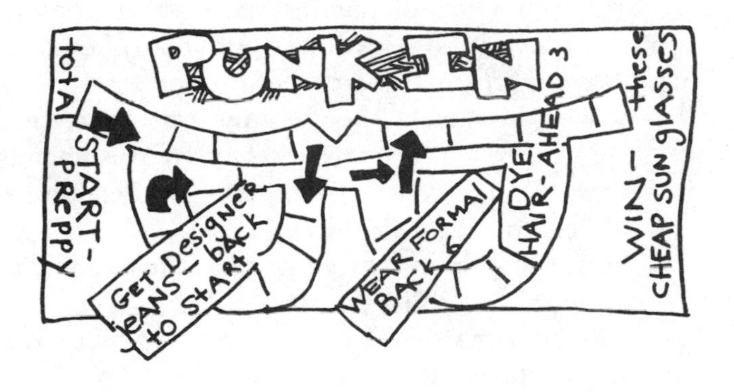

I quoted,

"Get old dress, ahead 3";
"Wear designer jeans, back to start";
"Dye hair extreme colors, ahead 6."

The finish reads, "You have won these cheap sunglasses."

"She's agreed to come one time to church with me and the children."

"Good luck." He laughed. "You are really going to

like Gloria, too. She will be here within two weeks."

From the wedding I remembered her as a tall blond girl who had been eager to help her father. She had sewn some buttons on his suitcoat and stayed with him until the ceremony.

"I've been talking with her. She wants to assist in the office and not take any college classes. When she gets here, I'm having her pick up a rental car at the airport as she will need her own transportation."

As Jeremy talked, I again experienced the feeling of anxiety at another stepdaughter coming. She would actually be closer to my age than I was to my husband's. This increasing number of people residing with us would add to the complexities of our marriage adaptations. Yet I reminded myself how Jessie had proved to be far less of a problem than I had feared before her arrival.

We sat in silence after Jeremy ordered coffee. Because it was our anniversary, I wanted to brush hands and interchange some dense cosmic rays of affection.

"I remember," said Jeremy.

I was instantly ready for that sled. My mind flew with his two words recalling Mexico. . . .

"When I married Patty, we were so poor that we couldn't even buy the wedding pictures."

This reminiscing would have been all right on another night of the year. I sat there listening about his first family, their trailer, baby Robert, and their anniversaries. My feelings were crushed, and my throat began to ache as I held back any cry.

I began to quietly crumble my fortune cookie, breaking off bits of it as he talked. I wouldn't even open its message slip, just stood to go leaving it still folded on the plate.

Jeremy followed me to the car. I thought, In all ways he is a most brilliant man, except in his management of a wife's emotional needs.

Once home, Jeremy fell asleep instantly. I wallowed in disappointment until humor rescued me with its own perspective. I whispered over at Jeremy's deaf ears:

"If I were involved in an accident, my husband would not be able to identify the body."

November 3

I was in the corridor of a dream. The image, with its mists and forms, enveloped my mind. At first I explained the sound of the tapping in colors that pulsed. But the sound broke through my sleep, chipping off pieces, making a hole of consciousness. The room was washed in the early morning color of pearl. As Jeremy called, "Come in," from the adjusted height of his elbow, I was ready to rebuke whatever child wanted to confide with us at dawn.

It wasn't a child at all, but Gloria, who had moved in earlier in the week. She walked over to the small table by her father's side holding the white coffeepot and single mug.

She had come from Minneapolis with numerous

taped boxes and suitcases. I had seen little of her, as she was working the same long hours as Jeremy.

My feeling of "Invasion at Daybreak" didn't lift. I burrowed deeper into the blankets wishing for the hole of sleep's gravity. I thought, It's her father's job to explain our personal territories and hours of access.

"You wanted to start early today, Jeremy."

I opened my eyes. It was the first time I noticed that Gloria called her father by his first name. My mind inventoried Jessie's vocabulary, thinking that this might be a part of the family government, but I could only remember the younger sister using the word "Dad."

Moving my head to focus, I looked at Gloria. She had on a long bathrobe made of a purple synthetic material. It appeared to be created from fuzz pulled off and compacted from blankets. Her hair hung down with the strands indented from the single French braid that she usually wore. It was her hands that commanded my attention. Her vermilion fingernails had the artificial sharp uniformity that's only possible when glued in place at beauty shops. I noted on her right hand that Gloria wore her mother's wedding ring.

Jeremy looked up at the digital clock that he kept on his dresser.

"Thank you," he said.

"It will soon be nine o'clock in New York."

"Look, folks, it's barely past five-thirty here," I stated.

Gloria turned, casting out a "See you later" at the door. Once alone, I had to make a statement.

"I hope this won't become a habit."

Jeremy bristled. "Look. Laurel, I couldn't ask for more efficiency or loyalty. Gloria's going to be the office manager and I've shared with you how she's helped me before."

I did remember. The first time Patty had moved out

of the family home, Gloria, who was then in high school, took over managing the two younger children. She had also lived with her dad when he first opened the L.A. office, and helped pick the personal furnishings for his condominium.

Jeremy's speech on her office efficiency made me visualize her in the downstairs shower typing with her finger pads on the yellow tile as an exercise to increase her words per minute. As Jeremy stood up, I could tell by his expression that he thought what was good for him, should be good for me, which is good for the world, and that should settle it.

But I couldn't let it rest. I was feeling agitated and uneasy, sensing the potential of a whole new sphere of conflict.

I had learned to speak as quietly as he did, but inside I was shaking my husband by the shoulders.

"I definitely feel Gloria needs her own apartment. It would be better for both your daughter and us."

He walked to the bathroom and picked up a towel from the shelf built into an alcove by the door. I suspected that he wanted to ignore the subject. Gloria's shower water was still coursing through the pipes which forced him to stand by the bathroom and wait. The house plumbing could only take care of one need at a time.

"You have your children here, and I have the equal right for all of mine to live with me if I want."

I knew there could be no reasoning with him, but I could feel glib anger begin providing sentences of accusation for my tongue to slip on. He had once stated that his children would never live with us, and he knew beforehand about mine.

I got out of bed and walked over to the window that faces the east. I looked at the morning light beginning to illuminate the grove of eucalyptus trees behind Jean La-Cour's house. I remembered when we moved in a year ago how I had imagined koala bears rollicking in the upper limbs. I wondered if it were possible to graph all of my whimsical thoughts and rate their decline into sobriety.

"I don't want to quarrel, Jeremy."

"Neither do I, Laurel."

Our truce seemed to be composed of one single flag that was more gray than white.

December 1

"Hello, Arlene. It's me again. Laurel."

I lay on the office rug holding the door shut with my foot. My niche at Summertree Productions had become a telephone booth with two WATS line buttons, allowing for long-distance calls at a reduced rate.

"I think I am going crazy!"

I envisioned a mental hospital built on one floor with adjacent gardens. I imagined being hospitalized and allowed to do one simple activity. I would use crayons in a coloring book, filling in one-dimensional drawings with little strokes.

Arlene's responding laughter was infectious. Maybe, I mused, I should mark this, too, as another sign of my mental decline: Laurel Lee will laugh at anything.

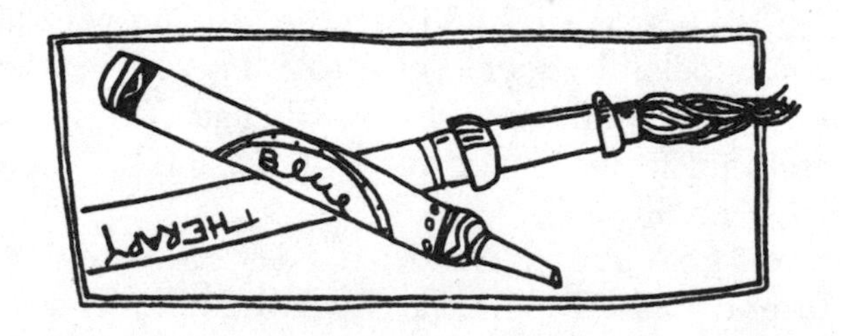

Moving into a sitting position, I put my back against the door and surveyed the room. In the months of secluding myself in the day's odd hours to keep a diary, all officelike appearances had been stripped away.

On the floor there had been a clear plastic piece cut with kidney-bean curves for a chair to roll on. It was the first thing that I had taken out into the storage room. In its place was a hand-loomed rug. I used baskets for filing cabinets. The stock boy had helped me tack a full-size quilt over a blank wall. I had found costumes left on a back rack from a movie filmed in India. I put some of the gauze and cotton pieces on the brass prongs of my coatrack. In the privacy of a mood I would dress in them, or wear them in layers whenever the air conditioning had been adjusted to blow the coldest drafts.

"Arlene, I've decided that marriage resembles a boating excursion. During courtship the suitor takes his seat in the bow, crooning with a ukulele, while the woman smooths the wrinkles from her gown. Then comes the current. Low hanging branches swipe at them, and there are rocks right below the surface that can easily tear a craft."

I limited my long-distance calls to three chosen women friends. They could be trusted. They had practiced for years keeping secrets in their church life. Their muscles of confidence had grown strong by keeping to themselves the personal disclosures of what girl was engaged and what wife was pregnant.

I only divulged a part of my difficulties to each one so it was three times as serious as any human thought.

Both Arlene and Margo heard mostly about my mental health. Since both of them were married, they understood the potential weight in a relationship's yoke. I described my mind to Arlene as some days feeling like a table with wads of old gum being pressed underneath it.

My friend liked specifics more than similes.

"How are your stepdaughters?"

"There is no descriptive phrase for Jessie other than that she is in the process of becoming. I took her to the high school and got her enrolled in studies with an art emphasis. She goes to class wearing Levis and 1950 felt hats with mesh net veils.

"Gloria is much more difficult. Toward me, her conduct is faultlessly polite, but it's marked by a tangible reserve and distance."

In turn, I listened. I liked news of a life. Her children were in music recitals, and her secret fear was that she had a receding hairline. But with Arlene, I could count on listening to advice. She has multiple vitamin words for a soul.

"Laurel, don't even indulge yourself in looking back to either the courtship flush or the days before you met Jeremy."

The fourth light dimmed on fifteen interoffice phones as I hung up. I took off the white Nehru jacket wishing Melanie wasn't outside leaning with her paint ladder against some Portland fish scale shingle. I felt like talking with every one of my support group friends. Instead, I picked up my purse to go home.

Even at the door's first crack was a sound wave of typewriters. Across from the receptionist's corridor, Jeremy's door was closed. He was on a business trip to a Texas city. Next to it, I could see Len's accounting assistant shuffling through a metal drawer along a wall of filing cabinets.

Gloria's desk was in the first carpeted area behind the women's rest room. She had before her a diet pop and an order of tortilla chips smothered in cheese. Her preference was to have her food brought in so she could work through lunch. While we greeted each other I saw she had mounted photos on her bulletin board. One was of herself dressed as a harem girl at a Halloween party. Another was Jeremy and Patty in blue ski sweaters, arm in arm. It seemed that all of her apparent loyalties were locked to the old order.

I walked out into the midday sun whose position put my shadow right under my feet.

December 4

Jessie took one of the girl's sunglasses off the dashboard and put them on. At the end of each frame was a grinning characterization of a chicken. While she tilted the rear-view mirror and peered at her reflection, I answered her question.

"Yes, you can wear them to school."

I asked Jessie where she would like to have lunch.

"Oh, pizza," was her quick reply.

Without allowing any natural pause she continued, "I knew Gloria wouldn't come when you asked us out to eat this morning. She's just like Dad, and has to work on Saturdays."

We were driving down a main street in the San Fernando Valley. Every block bore a sign for Mexican food with the letters adjacent to a painting of a cactus or sombrero. I calculated that there were two drive-thru houses for fast hamburgers per mile. Jessie changed her mind when she saw a red-and-white revolving bucket advertising a Kentucky Fried Chicken outlet.

At the counter she requested an additional salad, corn, and pudding. She was still young enough to have a passion of appetite without the restraint of considering calories.

Once in our booth Jessie asked me to tell her about one of my favorite moments in life. Her question had the ring of an English class writing assignment. I suspected she was trying to divert my attention from any questions that I might raise about school. There had been a call to the house from the attendance office informing me of recurring absences.

"Once I smuggled Bibles into the U.S.S.R."

"When?" she asked.

"Only three years ago," I replied, to her surprise.

I explained to Jessie how I was invited to join a tour of university teachers. The trip was scheduled during my season with chemotherapy, but the exact date was one of the weeks that I didn't have to have maintenance drugs.

While being drawn into my narration, I had stopped hearing the metallic droning of the video games and the restaurant's public music. I reached over and pulled off the tiny chicken glasses from Jessie's face, telling her it was my turn to wear them.

I went on to describe our landing in what looked like fields of snow. After passing through visa inspection, we got our luggage under an eight-foot oil painting of Lenin.

I told Jessie that the only thing modern about the airport was the baggage inspection. It resembled a grocery's gleaming checkout counter. Seeing the extent that the suitcases were being searched, I became afraid to attempt the smuggling.

"What were they doing?"

"Not only was every article of clothing being pulled out, but I saw inspectors have people remove their shoes to check that nothing was concealed between the sole and the leather."

It was my struggle with doubts that I detailed. Confiscation seemed more than probable. I feared that all the innocent passengers on my flight would be refused entrance into the country as punishment along with me. Because of the evident risks, I unzipped my suitcase and piled the books on a bench. When I turned to leave them and take my place in line, I found that I couldn't walk away.

"One truth that I experienced while fighting cancer is that nothing is impossible with God. Sometimes people who are expected to die one hour get up the next.

"So, Jessie, I simply put the Bibles back in my bag and stood in line."

"What happened?" she asked.

I described how I was manifesting every nervous symptom. My face was red. My palms were damp. The agent was meticulous in his inspection of the man in front of me.

When it was my turn, I thought I would faint from stress. I decided they would probably put me in jail with a sentence they could wag to others as a deterrent for transporting contraband.

With one arm's gesture, the inspector waved me through and then began pulling out every garment from the bags of the person behind me.

I told her about the tears and embraces of those that I finally gave the Bibles to.

"Look, Jessie, school is hard, doing what's right can be hard, but some day it becomes worth it."

She answered me with a look that moves the eyes in an arc. I knew it was time to talk about nothing more serious than analyzing the greasy fingerprints stamped along the table.

"How come you ever married Dad?" she asked. "It seems to me he never goes to church." She adjusted her statement while I said nothing.

"Oh, he went once since I've been here. It was the same Sunday there was company from his business."

I remembered how important it was to me when he told me it was his weekly practice.

"Maybe it's his intention," was my only reply.

It was hard to be quiet. "Now, Miss Jessie," I wanted to declare. She was sitting before me representing the young girls of the world. My thought seemed audible. "When the hour comes for considering matrimony, take the time to weigh the suitor's speeches against his conduct."

Instead, I gave her back the sunglasses. After wiping my hands with a napkin, I put the box of leftovers in a sack. I watched my stepdaughter walk out in front of me. I sighed that the human ear has such a small shelf within its curve for holding instructions.

January 5, 1982

Leaning against the deck's rail, I could hear the humming faucets as Julia filled the sink with detergent. I had glanced at the collection of china stained from the morning's use. There were the youngest children's plates with catsup blobs from scrambled eggs, the Foster girls' saucers that they had appropriated as ashtrays, and Jeremy's coffee tray.

The fantasy of having a maid was over. I had found Julia another canyon family who wanted the services of a housekeeper as soon as I would release her. We had all agreed to a week.

As for me, I needed labor. There was a simple ther-

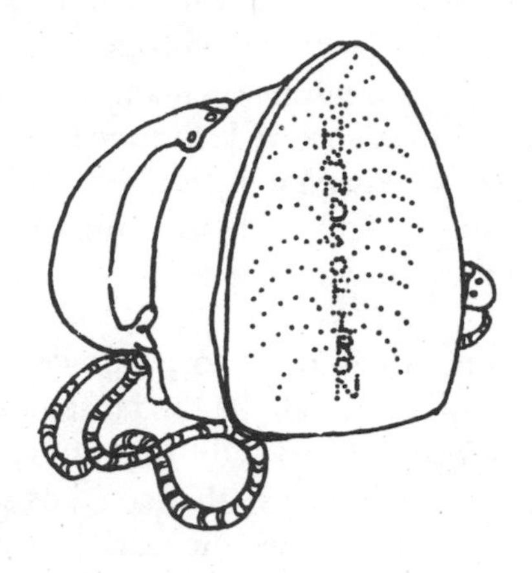

apy in scrubbing a bathtub with cleanser that turned blue when contacting water, and sweeping dust into piles. There was a sense of connection in knowing the contents of every covered dish in the icebox. The children, too, were getting lazy. They needed chores far more than having them performed by a hired adult.

I had also learned that too much solitude produced introspection, and too much analysis tended toward melancholy.

I pinched off bits of bread crust for the birds, scattering crumbs along the rail. The bluejays moved between branches, their heads cocked at attention to the bounty. I reflected that having a maid had given me lots of time to write. Shaking out the rest of the bread sack, I felt an appreciation for the season Jeremy had provided. I thought of my pen at the office as an iron with which I could press my feelings onto a page. Yet I sensed that I had disappointed Jeremy. He had given me books to read with the instruction to try and turn them into scripts. In every attempt I choked all of the necessary action with metaphors. I was born too late for the age of radio showcase drama.

I took the far stairs built of mortared brick to start my descent to the back of the property. Roots and ground swells gave each tread its own angle. Thirty railroad ties followed the masonry as I clumped down in my open-heeled clogs. I crossed a hillside pad of knee-high weeds to a single pine. I had taken the time for the private quiet known to those in cloisters or caves. No one could hear me.

It was my daily need to go down to the back acre. I felt exactly like a watch that had lost its accuracy and had to stand before God for adjustment. There were days I had resentments to bring, that acted as sand grains clogging my works. In prayer, the ticking of pain has a potential for release.

Part of my care was the whole situation with Jessie. She had denied that she knew where certain items of clothing and jewelry were. The child had just started disappearing for a few days and then would show up with a strange explanation. She had lost Matthew's sleeping bag when she said she was kidnapped on the beach.

But it was Jeremy and Gloria who perplexed me. Their solution was to falsify our home address in order to transfer Jessie to a high school near the production office. The child's presence was required after 4:00 P.M. to sort papers for the minimum wage.

"You can't correct her for lying by lying yourself," I had protested.

"And this will be boring to her. I know she'll run away."

I ranged from thoughts back to prayer.

I know God tempers the wind that's blown over the shorn lamb.

"Even so, blow here."

I reflected on how my husband himself was changing. He was burrowing even deeper into work. His one expression of rest on Sunday was now spent at Summertree Productions. For Christmas Gloria had just bought him a new television that was the size of one of his office shelves. Now he could watch Sunday sports from his padded desk chair.

I thought of it as a new glaze of silence to Jeremy Foster. He was a back to me at night, and by day only exhibited a kind of sealed inner eye.

I remembered how Arlene said there were some in Portland who wished they had my maid, house on a hill, and a husband in a Mercedes-Benz. I had to give a short laugh, thinking that outside appearances rarely tell the scale of the battle.

I leaned over to one side in the pine needles and looked out at the sky. I sang for myself:

Come unto Me
You who are heavy laden
And I will give you rest.

Even so, blow here.

January 14

I left my car at the office parking lot in response to Jeremy's invitation for breakfast.

"Doesn't the interior look good?"

He brushed his hand across the leather hearth above the steering wheel. I nodded my assent.

"Gloria found some special waxes for automotive interiors and spent Sunday morning hand-rubbing them in."

It was only a few blocks from the office to the Breakfast Cottage, a restaurant with the peaked roof of a home over its central sign.

Jeremy was vigorous in sprinkling pepper grains over the surface of the eggs, while I ate my bagel with feigned appetite. It was unusual for me to be invited in midmorning for a meal. I wondered if he had any reason other than us having some time together like a handshake. There was a hum of language from the dining booths that outlined the side of our room. It was the talk of toast crumbs and coffee cup saucers. I felt the drowsiness that poor air and warmth produces.

Jeremy said he had a problem.

Instantly, I was alert. It was his quiet voice where one word doesn't weigh any more in a spoken sound than another. He had rehearsed some disclosure.

"It's a frailty."

He was pausing now with his phrase that was a synonym for the weakness in human nature.

"I just—it's just a lack of emotional attachment for you."

He spread out his hands. They were open and empty.

I felt myself being pierced. Physical pain can never approximate the anguish in a spirit.

"It's something I've been strugging with a long time, and it's caused me a lot of suffering too."

I could have comforted him if he had grief from any other cause but this. Instead, I sat completely mute from the shock of his statement. While Jeremy paid the cashier, I walked by him and out to the parking lot. Waiting by the locked door, I stood in a state of fierce aloneness. Neither of us spoke, and the front car seat was miles long for our distance. Once Jeremy had pulled between the white lines by the company door, he turned to me again.

"Look, there's still love without any emotional connectors."

"Sure," I replied with sarcasm. "You love divinity fudge and Abe Lincoln too."

He shrugged, not comprehending me, and went inside the production office. I wondered why he couldn't see the hurt trying to get its giant form behind my pointed picket fence.

I just went over to my station wagon and sat behind the steering wheel. Looking down I saw that every indentation in the floor mats was filled with sand. There was also a green crayon, an orange juice cap, one safety pin, a peso, and a grocery receipt. Then I gave my first cry in one deep sound. I couldn't turn on the ignition. His loss of love for me explained all those weeks that had been marked by such painful distances. He had gone from the ardor of courtship to the routines of daily responsibilities, to what he termed "a lack of emotional attachment."

His words seemed like a rock thrown into a pond. Upon impact, successive rings were appearing in the water, round after round. The first wave was anguish for myself, followed by sorrow for the children. Then, I was mourning for those alive and suffering, and those who have, and those who will. The history of the world was in tears.

The girls were in the driveway. Anna's school sack was abandoned by the door. She and Mary Elisabeth were occupied with searching for the sun lizards that darted around the clay pots. Watching them gave me some consolation that they had never seemed affected by all the change. They remained essentially cheerful.

"Why don't you ever bring home some doughnuts?" Anna said.

I pointed for them to look up at two doves sitting on a utility wire. When one flew away, I found myself earnestly wishing it would come back and land by the other.

Once in the front door, I found Matthew had brought in the mail to the front hall table. I glanced at the free newspaper of ads. It was headlined "HOME IMPROVEMENTS NEEDED."

My pain could turn everything into a message. I could be vulnerable to song lyrics and the Feeler Fortunes inserted in bubble gum wrappers.

When Jeremy came home, I was waiting for him in the kitchen.

I had thought of words that I hoped would string some lights in our relationship's darkness. I had practiced them until my voice was without emotional timbre.

"I appreciate that you were just being honest this morning in telling me your struggle to feel an attachment to me. For months I have been thinking about marriage relationships."

Jeremy put some ice in a cup and got some water from the sink. He sat at the window and crossed his cowboy boots.

"I've decided that one essence of love is the fact that it is not something we have to always feel. It's more of an attitude and a conduct."

"You're just going to take your twenty-six letters and lay words on me," he replied.

Here was my husband who could quote the time in every city of the world. He alone made decisions and carried weights that usually rested on whole institutions. I wanted us to stand again arm in arm.

"Oh, Jeremy, let's get marriage counseling. We have both helped a lot of people, but maybe this is the time we need help ourselves."

"You can," he hissed. "I'm going to bed."

Both heat and emotion rise faster than logic. As he pursed his lips to walk past me, his silence seemed worse than a parting word.

"Won't you talk with me?" I cried.

He used a voice that was so quiet it seemed to come from the stillness that rides in the center of the storm.

"I'm not going to cast out my pearls. . . ." he said.

My mind instantly filled in the last two words he omitted. They were from a scripture line that ended with the phrase, swine. His choice of speech pierced me like a dart.

My immediate wound wouldn't let me sit still enough to hear a choir sing. I had run out of cheeks to turn. In less than a second I tightened my fingers into a fist and punched his upper arm. My knuckles hit the area of flesh where doctors give vaccinations. He grabbed my assailing hand by the wrist.

I saw myself through his eyes as a kind of wild woman dipping into conduct that was out of control. I felt both shame and pain. I had never hit anyone before. It was shame that apologized.

When I finally crawled next to his sleeping side knowing he had no regard for me, it was a Hindu bed of spikes.

There was no release in sleep. A parade of dreams began, each with its own colored float. One was the dove still alone on the wire. Another was my wedding bouquet with every flower dry and flammable. I dreamed a key was being inserted in our front door lock and someone said, "Is there a family in the house?"

I was in ancient Cana running back from the kitchen to the guests at the wedding supper, saying, "We have run out of wine."

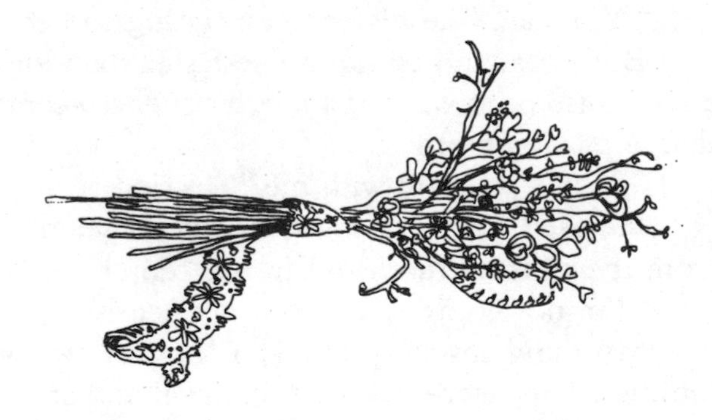

January 15

My analysis would not stop ticking and talking to me. I coveted a simple mind.

One of the little girls had taken my brush out of our

medicine chest and brought it into their children's bathroom. In their mirror's reflection I watched this middle-thirties woman pull all the hair back from her face and secure it with an elastic. My gray hairs were like leaves changing color for another season.

Boiling away every hurt and accusation made the issue very simple: I wanted to love and be loved. In all our high-wire acts of adaptation, I had never doubted the base of Jeremy's affection. It had been a fact that had helped me to keep trying and make adjustments. Now, by his own words, he was rolling our safety net away. I felt afraid.

Out the window, I could see the morning mist lying in pockets in the crevices of the hills. I took one deep breath and went back into our bedroom.

Jeremy sat on the bed, changing the television channels with a remote-control device. He weaved the warp of the screen with strands from every network's news. I interrupted a foreign journalist's report on Beirut.

"Jeremy, I've designed a daytime game program. It's called 'I Don't Get No Respect.' It will have a panel of wives, each allowed a specific time to relate their marital problems. The audience will vote by applause at who's the most ill treated, and the winner gets a ticket for one to a resort."

Jeremy laughed as I continued.

"Any tie between contestants will be settled by a telephone call, amplified for the audience, to the ex-wife."

"And her prize," Jeremy added, "will be a check for double her month's alimony."

"Look," I said while turning off the television. "I've been around commercials for a long time. What is it that you don't like about me, itchy dandruff flakes, these horrid age spots?" I held up the back of my hand.

All of a sudden the walls seemed to sweat for seriousness. Jeremy stood up in a valley of decision. I felt he wouldn't lie to me—as wonderful or terrible as that could be. He could begin to stitch us together or rend us apart by his answer.

I spoke again.

"We all have blind spots in the perception of ourselves. I'm motivated to change."

After a prolonged pause, Jeremy replied.

"I cannot stand how you are always so intense, always ardent; you repeat yourself, and everything to you is a holy cause."

The hope in me began to bolt. If there were a machine that took X rays of a personality so its structure could be visible, I was intense. It went back to the months that the amniotic waters hid my form.

"And," he added in a softer voice, "you don't have any desire for accomplishing things. . . ."

He was wrong. But I couldn't find the words to explain my idea of progress as being internal and invisible.

Jeremy stopped looking at me and gazed out at the mountains.

"I am tired of any kind of demands. Look, Laurel, I know that I'm too much of an independent person for marriage. I really knew it the first time."

His shoulders seemed to roll a fraction forward. "I've thought a lot about it."

His eyes stayed on the hills. "The important thing is to take care of this in a way that won't cast a shadow on either of our reputations. No divorce. We'll just separate, and I'll get you the kind of house that you would like back in Oregon.

"We'll continue to make any necessary public appearances together."

I knew he meant those times when Mr. and Mrs. Foster were invited again as guests on a national Christian network, or to the President's prayer breakfast.

The hypocrisy of his proposal made me look hard at him. His words reminded me of a tomb. The appearance was whitewashed and ornate, but inside were skeleton shards. *Words are always a second face.*

"It's just like making movies to you, isn't it, Jeremy? Everything has to be for image and nothing for substance."

I raised my voice. "You don't seem to care about imitating what is good, only how to counterfeit it."

A terrible silence filled the room. I had just displayed every characteristic that he had enumerated, besides a few more. My voice dropped.

"I will not live a lie. And I will not leave you either."

He had become as stern and fierce as I had ever seen him. He answered me in a thunder peal.

"I'll keep this room then, and you can sleep on the other side of the house by your children!"

Julia's bed had been empty for just over a week.

I studied Jeremy's face, not trusting myself to speak. Either rage or hurt would want to further oil the hinges of my mouth.

If "lack of attachment" were a creature all its own, it had shed its skin, revealing features marked by hostility. I stood there, not knowing how to leave the bedroom. It was now a territory that was neither "ours" nor "mine."

Only by thinking of a sculpture of an Indian I once saw could I walk to the door. He sat on a horse with a spear buried in his chest, but instead of being stooped over, his hands and face were raised to the sky.

January 17

It wasn't the sound of the shower running that woke me, but the silence directly after it was turned off. My twin bed was above the kitchen. Soon I could hear Gloria take the whistling kettle off the burner to pour the water through the filter. She carried the coffee tray up the stairs to her father. Every morning she used the same soft knock at the door.

I stared at the wallpaper, knowing that my step-daughter was seeing that I had been expelled from the room. I felt my face flush that such a close-range observer could see our troubles. I didn't want to imagine even a line of their dialogue. I made it a forbidden thought.

I needed a devotion, feeling starved for daily bread, feeling I couldn't get my eyes high enough to see the hills from whence cometh my help. I chose one line and held it steady while tracing the wallpaper's miniature bright stars embossed on blue.

My impulse was to write, using my pen as alchemy for changing the baser circumstances into words. As a journal keeper, I wanted to divert some pain into language, but remembered that my diary was still at the office.

It wasn't until the afternoon, when I was bent in my chores, that I thought about the money. I was in the process of trying to roll the rubber garter down on a new vacuum cleaner bag. Stopping all work, I realized that because of my trust in my husband, I had taken all of my separate property earned before marriage and put it in a community account. It had not been done all at once. First was the balance in my checking and savings passbooks, then the Treasury certificates as they matured.

I stood up to calculate. There were the additional cash assets from the sale of two houses that I had given my husband to deposit. It was Jeremy who had asked for both of them to be sold. Abandoning the old Hoover, I went to look for our current account number in my purse.

One grief was that never before had I doubted Jeremy's financial integrity. All numbers, bills, forms, and taxes belonged to his talent. He knew the zip codes for America. He could quote the populations of small towns in the Midwest.

I didn't bother with the yellow pages, but waited through the sixty-second recording that suggests to Los Angeles residents that they keep better phone records. I gave the information operator our bank and branch, then dialed the seven digits into the North Hollywood Bank of America.

I imagined that the institution's officer only had to twirl a knob and look into a lighted computer screen. She stated an amount less than two thousand dollars. I thanked her, marveling at the polite composure that's possible when layers of the earth are shaking. More than one hundred thousand dollars were gone.

I tried immediate reassurance, suggesting to myself that Summertree Productions has its own account. But I felt my mental paragraph to be mock and frail. It seemed to me that I had no alternative but to confront Jeremy at his office, the center arena of his business.

There was no color left to evening when I could finally take my car keys in hand. Driving to town, I felt I had the sweat of an ancient soldier. It wasn't a state of dread, but a feeling of being dispatched for defense when one's town has been looted. The bulk of that money was an estate for my children. We had always lived simply; it was Jeremy who was extravagant.

Only my husband's car was in the lot. Gloria liked to take a few hours at a health spa before following her father home. Someone had forgotten to lock the warehouse door. I walked through the darkness to the lights at the front offices. I could hear Jeremy's television, but at his doorway saw that his back was to the screen. He had on his glasses, a short-sleeved shirt, and was bent over a trade magazine.

"Hello, it's me," I said.

His reply was equally cordial. He rose to his feet, not in greeting, but just to face me.

I looked at his room. It was where he received many of his prospective film investors. It could have belonged to a theologian for the number of its Bible-related pictures and verses. The back wall was entirely books. Some were leather-bound prayers, and others, sermon principles. I didn't want to forget my diary, and decided to get it first, before beginning any discussion.

As I turned, Jeremy walked quickly after me.

"I thought it was best to make a change," he said. His voice had an anxious pitch.

He was right if he was anticipating my hysteria. When I turned on the light, everything of mine was gone. The quilt, baskets, library table, and rug had been replaced by standard office equipment. One desk faced the door, and another was set at the side. Both had typewriters.

"I moved Gloria in here," Jeremy said.

My impulse was to run and cry. I wanted to put the children in the car and find an Oregon cave to call home. I wanted anything where there could be peace and order.

I knew I was shaking.

"Where is all that money, Jeremy?"

He shut the office door while giving me a shrug.

"You, of your own free will, put it in a joint account."

How I understood the anger of Christ when He called,

> *You hypocrites who will devour a widow's purse and for a pretense, make a long prayer.*

I followed Jeremy into the warehouse after he had switched on the lights. I could see my brass coatrack protruding from a box near the door. The oval basket was next to it with the quilt folded over the top. I couldn't stop myself from fluttering with tears, and taking breaths that shook in my chest. Jeremy walked to the rear door and loaded my possessions into the hatchback of my station wagon.

I drove up into the colder air of the canyon. My rage knotted my ideas into the same cord that Jesus used on certain businessmen in the temple. He overturned tables and the seats of those who sold doves.

Jeremy Foster was now a wolf to me. He had an elongated jaw. His closet was filled with sheepskins which he knew how to fit over every claw.

After expending myself in thoughts, I became sober and still. It was only my desire for my diary that gave me the strength to pull the things into the house from the back of the car. I felt I had words backing up past my wrist, into my arm.

I brought in the large basket last and pulled off the quilt. Only the rug was underneath it. All of my papers were gone. I couldn't find my spiral theme books filled with notes of our married months. If it was an intentional act of disposal, they looked exactly like diary records.

But my journal was safe. It had been concealed by my haphazard filing system. I always kept it hanging from the coatrack deep within a woven peasant's bag.

Taking it out, I scribbled in a margin,

That I might withstand these days,
and having done all, to stand.

January 26

I knew that my resolve was crumbling. The days seemed like seawater trying to wash out the mortar in my walls. The battering on the outside was taking its toll, but the damage was the dampness that crept within.

I barely saw Jeremy and Gloria, except in the mornings. It was as if they took a strict vow of silence when passing by me in the kitchen, or walking past me in the hall. Their meditation seemed audible; they wanted us to leave.

I sat on the stairs, marveling at Jeremy's stamina for dissension. I felt the ghosts from his first relationship's separation. It seemed to me that a second marriage can never change the past as much as reveal it. Pulling my knees up to my chin, I could feel my need for a resting-place apart from the extreme tensions in the house.

Going down to the kitchen phone I dialed the area code for the Silvercreek Falls retreat center. In minutes the wire of the ringing telephone stretched into acres of Oregon fir trees.

Pastor Hanson answered. He had pronounced our matrimonial vows over us.

"Well, yes," was his immediate reply when I asked for a room. He explained that the two lodges were booked through the winter for conferences.

"If you don't mind a small trailer, there is one up on the hill you can use."

I felt as if I had been living in a boxing arena and needed the corner of the ring. There would be water and a towel. I couldn't guess the time it would take between bells.

Having forgotten to put on slippers, my bare feet were cold from standing on the clay tiles. The floor had absorbed January's air. Pulling a stool over to the phone, I dialed Topanga Elementary School. I wished ardently it were summer vacation for the children, whose school classes were progressing into winter term. The receptionist used a Southern California vocabulary. After my vague and brief statements on withdrawing the three of them, she wanted to know if I were taking them with me "on location." It was the only school I knew where the mothers wore pink bib overalls and woolly exercise socks to PTA meetings. Last month's function included an art exhibit of the parents' work.

I knew I would have to tell Jeremy my plan. Phoning his office, I hoped he would be able to take my call. His voice warmed as I mentioned going to Oregon. He had one instruction.

"Work with a realtor to find a house that you and the children could move into. I would be willing to get a moving company and ship you your personal furniture."

His words brought back to me the feeling of being an Indian ordered from the tribal lands to find a reservation.

Mary Elisabeth brought into the packed car a blue construction-paper hand fastened to a foot-long stick. She had created it at school, and it had fingernails shaped like stars. Using it as a wand, she waved "good-bye" to our house while I backed the station wagon from the driveway.

She turned her attention to Jean LaCour's carport and the row of mailboxes on their posts.

Anna suggested we make one stop in Topanga before going on the highway. She wanted to go by Gus McFadden's barn on the state parkland and look again at the baby winter goats. I explained that we couldn't as it

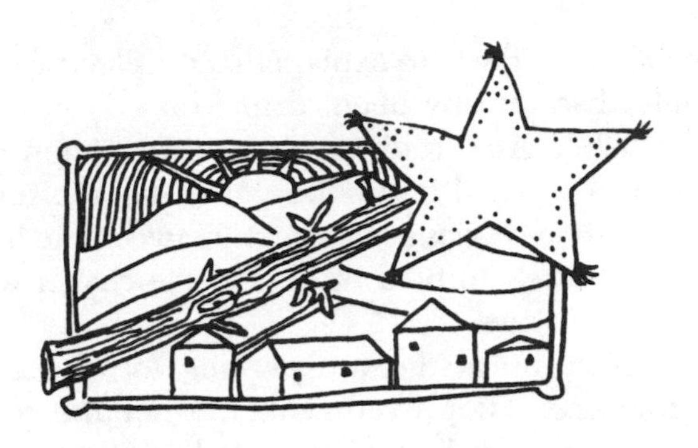

was going to take three days of driving to get to our camp in Oregon.

January 29

Once out of Salem, the country roads were built to go around fields, unlike the six-lane freeway that went straight through them. There was snow. It wasn't the thick drifts of winter calendar photos, but the faintest etching of white on the land that mostly stood in shadow through the day. I wanted to drink from the view through the dashboard window. There was no pleasure in looking around that car as it had disintegrated into a disordered clutter through the miles.

Matthew was in the front. He was already asking if he could drive once we turned onto the gravel logging road that led near to the center. There was a grocery bag crumpled at his feet and three skeleton apple cores on the small shelf behind the shift.

Our last stretch was a single lane. I could remember it in summers rich with foxgloves and daisies. Opening the window for a moment, I breathed in the cold of the afternoon.

Both Alan and Eunice Hanson were home. Part of

their greeting was to explain that the electric heater in the trailer had already been turned on.

While Alan told me the exact location of our new abode, I realized it was the trailer that the summer cook had lived in. It was at a point in between the house where I had dressed to be a bride and the chapel where I had taken my vows.

Once up at the top parking lot, the children ran before me. They lived with the impulse to race. Our hours in the car had only wound up the springs in their legs which were waiting for release. The front of the trailer rested on cement blocks and ends of boards. It had a faded decal of a bull's horns near the roof. It read, "Trails West."

Anna, the first inside, turned to announce it had a musty smell.

"But where will we all sleep?" Matthew asked.

There was a cubical for eating, two twin beds, and a quarter of a bathroom with a foot pedal for flushing the toilet. I showed them how to collapse the table's leg and unfold the dining seats to make another width for our sleeping bags.

I looked at the slick blond paneling and orange rubber-backed carpet. I pronounced it to be far better than our wide home with its strife.

"You hit your husband?"

I sat alone with Eunice Hanson in her living room. The dessert plates were still on the table. Her husband had just taken the children over to the lodge to go through a box of coats and sweaters left from the weeks of summer sessions. Mary Elisabeth had wanted to inventory the toys and borrow one from a box in the nursery.

To Eunice's question I had to nod my head "yes." Her expression bordered on unbelief. I felt like the girl from childhood's poem.

When she was good, she was very good,
but when she was bad, she was horrid.

Eunice's voice was gentle.

"What are the ways you differ from the person that Jeremy thought he was marrying?"

It was asked to give me a point of meditation and did not require any paragraph of reply.

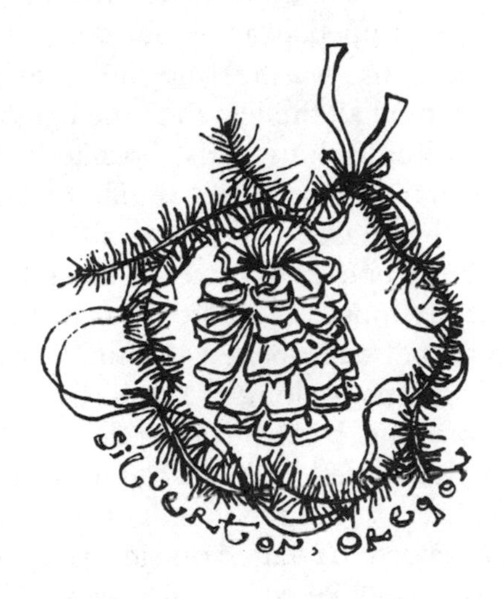

Using my headlights was the only possible way to get back to our trailer. Clouds blotted every star. There was a penetrating dampness with the silence of the woods. It was the kind of night when fallen leaves are absorbed into the ground's wet mulch.

Once we were all zipped into our single flannel bags, I listened to the children breathing. Their sound reminded me of a factory for manufacturing sleep. Because of the number of my thoughts, I knew it would be hours before I could join their production line.

I had begun analyzing my two marital relationships.

My first husband had moved into our babysitter's house when I was in the hospital, and now my life savings were gone and my second husband was trying to force me to move out of state. I felt like a tree that lightning had struck twice.

Restless, I sat up and found my tennis shoes in the dark. Already wearing a sweatshirt and sweat pants, I wrapped my sleeping bag around me as a thick robe. Stepping outside, I stood insulated from feeling any cold. My sight was stripped away by our being in a dark forest. My strongest sense was hearing the night sounds. There was a soft rain on all the leaves at the heights of branches receding back into the woods. I walked a few feet from the door listening to my feet shuffle on the gravel.

Through the trees I could finally see one light at a staff member's house. My breath turned to the briefest mist about my mouth. I walked down the short trail toward the chapel and opened the single side door. Running my finger pads along the wall, I felt my way to the inset box of lights by the double doors. The one switch I touched illuminated bulbs placed in the ceiling to shine upon the altar. I could see them again out the window as the instant reflection created outside a second church with a quality of lines like rooms in dreams. There were no pews. A stack of folding chairs was leaning against one of the walls.

The rug was almost startling for its bright shade of red. It seemed like part of a devotion, that it was one of the three colors by which all colors are made.

I walked to the front. The altar was built of wood as thick as half a tree. On it was a single crucifix. I couldn't stop the memory of the last time I had stood there. The new Mr. and Mrs. Foster were being crowned in a final pastoral prayer over their union.

Now, I traced through my mind the utterance from the cross,

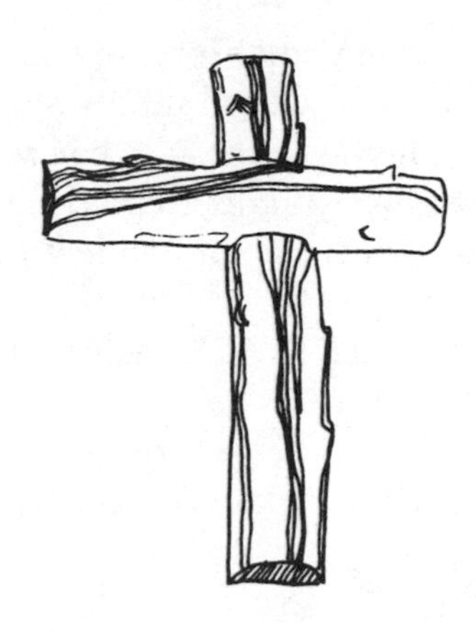

My God, why have you forsaken me?

I envisioned each letter separate and unconnected. Each was upper case and embellished with curlicues that trailed off into all the contradictions that had been endured.

I wished for a cathedral to trace the passion in stained glass. I imagined the act of refusing the bitter drink, which I pictured as a raised cup spilling over the sides with the memory of every act that caused hurt.

A realization can come suddenly into the mind. Some thoughts seem like moments suspended from time while their truth is grasped.

In drinking from the bitter waters of my own betrayal, it was clear that I was poisoning myself. I was always sipping on details.

There was no stopping Calvary's line.

Forgive them. They don't know what they are doing.

I didn't want to imagine any more, either in word or image. Wrapping my sleeping bag around me closer, I turned to go outside. My anger compared to having a tooth that hurt when any pressure was exerted against its enamel side. My tongue would always move to that corner of my mouth and touch it. I knew if I kept it, all my teeth would finally rot and I could never smile.

So it was torn from me while I cried:

I FORGIVE JEREMY FOSTER.

I felt as if I weighed nothing. I walked back to the trailer experiencing a cloud-base height above the rain.

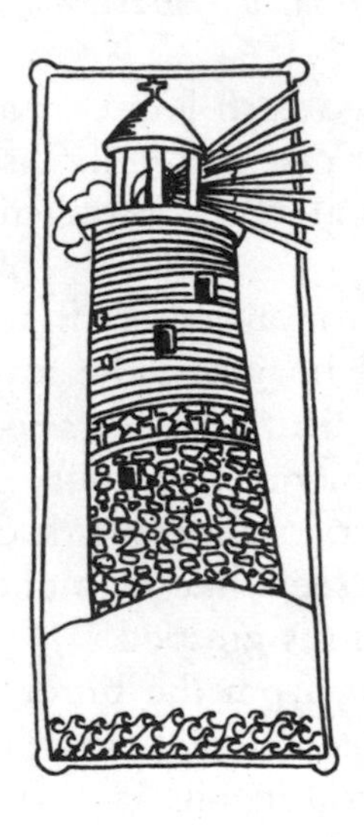

Portland, February 1

"What are you going to do now, Laurel?"

"Well, go immediately back to Topanga and be genuinely cheerful to every citizen in the hall. It's what I'm supposed to do."

I sat with Arlene in her living room. She had inherited some of her grandmother's furniture. Every piece was arranged in such close proximity that a feeling of confidentiality was lent to every sentence.

I told her how I had called the office to tell Jeremy I was coming back. He responded by not saying very much at all. His few words seemed more indifferent to my news than angry.

"I know it's going to be hard. But there is one important difference between the day I left and now. I don't see Jeremy as my opponent."

I explained that once I had discovered that the money was gone, I suspected him of calculating the courtship for his own gain. *People* magazine had printed my entire finances in an issue simultaneous with his first visit.

"I now know that wasn't right. The expression of his feelings was genuine."

Arlene handed me a cup. It was an old flowered mug painted with English buttercups. As she poured the tea I thought how feelings can be deception's field. It had been easy for me to perceive Jeremy at first as having every virtue. Then, after prolonged familiarity, my knight in shining armor took on the character traits of villains.

"He was neither as good nor as bad as I saw him."

"Also," Arlene added, "Jeremy thought he was marrying a success-oriented professional, and you're not."

Her sentence made me imagine Jeremy looking at a briefcase in my hand. The lines of the bag wavered, as it expanded in form and changed before him into a common grocery sack.

I sipped from my drink after testing its temperature. Its steam warmed my cheeks.

I knew I had to consider and admit my own faults. There were lots of times I didn't bridle my tongue. But before words, and before attitudes, lay my real failing. It was prior to meeting Jeremy Foster. I paused in my probing. In wanting to be married, I had cried too long, and too often, for a husband. It was my dream that I had clenched in a fist of discontent and wouldn't release. But time had now pried every finger open. There is peace in an open and upraised hand that isn't grasping for anything.

"Through this, Arlene, I believe I'm learning to be content in whatever state I'm in."

My friend sat down next to me, abandoning her seat across the room.

"By all the evidence, Laurel, it does seem that Jeremy will move away. But until that hour, there is hope his commitment can revive."

I nodded in agreement. We both knew families where dead relationships had been restored. She touched my arm, then continued.

"You can't carry the responsibility for what he alone decides."

While my friend spoke I thought of Jeremy Foster as a clipper ship. He was resplendent in pennants and sails. But his direction had nothing to do with his banners, only with the hidden rudder of his own will.

I answered Arlene slowly.

"By coming into my life, he could not complete me. And if he should leave, it cannot defeat me."

My eye traced some of Arlene's labors at the other end of the room. A shirt that she was sewing for her husband was set on the back of a chair. One sleeve in matching material lay on the table. I knew I had to go. Arlene taught piano lessons and one of her students would soon be coming up the walk.

Once on the porch I saw that the rain had stopped. Isolated drops from the morning's deluge fell from branches. I crossed the yard looking up at the tree limbs ranging above my head. Their lines seemed sealed into winter, but I knew that within every twig were factories for leaves.

By the time I reached the driveway my feet were wet. Right next to my car door was a ladder leaning upright against the garage siding. It wasn't the colors of the paint stains that I stopped to study, but the rungs. My eye was set for seeing symbols. I imagined the ladder fixed to the earth, extending into the air and out of sight. I let words cross it, swaddled in clouds.

Call unto Me, and I will answer you,
and show you great and mighty things
that you know not yet.

Turning to go, I noticed that the wind was blowing over houses, across streets and lawns to the south.

Publisher's Note

On April 1, Jeremy Foster took all of his personal effects from the family home. When he refused to disclose where he was moving, Laurel Lee recorded in her diary:

> It seemed like the Middle Ages when common knowledge held that the world was flat. As Jeremy rounded the last turn, he could have been dropping off the edge of the known continent.

In a personal document drafted before his departure, Jeremy deeded the Topanga Canyon house to Laurel. At the time of the title transfer the property was in legal foreclosure proceedings due to delinquent house payments and a past-due balloon payment.

Through the help of Laurel's parents the property was able to be refinanced and saved.

> I rolled up my sleeves and walked through the rooms viewing them as a small herd of dairy cattle. They simply had to give milk. I advertised some of the bedrooms as available for part-time rentals.
>
> A computer expert moved into the guesthouse. Every Sunday she wore white gloves and rang bells in a church orchestra.
>
> An elderly British couple took the master bedroom. They used my teapot as an hour hand to mark their day.
>
> Visiting professors took over the property for the summer months. All desks and tabletops were covered with their pages detailing mathematical sums.

As of this writing Jeremy Foster lives in the Los Angeles area and operates Summertree Productions as president. He refused all options of marital counseling. A divorce was final in the autumn of 1983.

Gloria Foster continues to manage the film distribution business for her father.

Jessie Kay Foster returned to her mother's home in Minnesota, then left to join a city commune. She is now developing an art technique using an airless paint sprayer as her medium.

For the publication of this private journal the publisher has substituted fictitious names only for Laurel's husband, his family, and the title of his film company business.

Laurel Lee, with her three children, still lives in Topanga Canyon. There continues to be no evidence of Hodgkin's disease.

I think of the past as an elongated stretching bar. Often I cried from exertion. But now that all my mourning has passed, I have found that those years composed a stringent class of dancing lessons.

Now, I feel full of high leaps and balanced twirling. I'm experiencing the real joy that walks lightly on her toes.

Laurel is currently making application to teach overseas in a third world school. The Lee children, along with their mother, are hoping to move to an isolated district where horses are the common means of transportation.

CHRISTIAN HERALD ASSOCIATION AND ITS MINISTRIES

CHRISTIAN HERALD ASSOCIATION, founded in 1878, publishes The Christian Herald Magazine, one of the leading interdenominational religious monthlies in America. Through its wide circulation, it brings inspiring articles and the latest news of religious developments to many families. From the magazine's pages came the initiative for CHRISTIAN HERALD CHILDREN and THE BOWERY MISSION, two individually supported not-for-profit corporations.

CHRISTIAN HERALD CHILDREN, established in 1894, is the name for a unique and dynamic ministry to disadvantaged children, offering hope and opportunities which would not otherwise be available for reasons of poverty and neglect. The goal is to develop each child's potential and to demonstrate Christian compassion and understanding to children in need.

Mont Lawn is a permanent camp located in Bushkill, Pennsylvania. It is the focal point of a ministry which provides a healthful "vacation with a purpose" to children who without it would be confined to the streets of the city. Up to 1000 children between the age of 7 and 11 come to Mont Lawn each year.

Christian Herald Children maintains year-round contact with children by means of a *City Youth Ministry.* Central to its philosophy is the belief that only through sustained relationships and demonstrated concern can individual lives be truly enriched. Special emphasis is on individual guidance, spiritual and family counseling and tutoring. This follow-up ministry to inner-city children culminates for many in financial assistance toward higher education and career counseling.

THE BOWERY MISSION, located at 227 Bowery, New York City, has since 1879 been reaching out to the lost men on the Bowery, offering them what could be their last chance to rebuild their lives. Every man is fed, clothed and ministered to. Countless numbers have entered the 90-day residential rehabilitation program at the Bowery Mission. A concentrated ministry of counseling, medical care, nutrition therapy, Bible study and Gospel services awakens a man to spiritual renewal within himself.

These ministries are supported solely by the voluntary contributions of individuals and by legacies and bequests. Contributions are tax deductible. Checks should be made out either to CHRISTIAN HERALD CHILDREN or to THE BOWERY MISSION.